JACKSON'S TOWN

JACKSON'S TOWN

The Story of the Creation of West Hartlepool
and
the Success and Downfall of its Founder,

RALPH WARD JACKSON

Including the Battle for Christ Church

by ERIC WAGGOTT

PUBLISHED BY
HARTLEPOOL BOROUGH COUNCIL
1980

ISBN 0 9501306 1 3

Filmset in 11 point 'Monophoto' Times on 13 point body
by Northumberland Press Ltd,
Gateshead, Tyne and Wear
Printed and bound in Great Britain by
Fakenham Press Ltd,
Fakenham, Norfolk

Contents

List of Illustrations

Author's Preface

Insofar as it relates events and reproduces letters and documents, the story in this book is true. Where it expresses opinions, they are no less fallible than are most opinions.

Much of it was known by a few people more than a hundred years ago but has not been passed on to present or recent generations.

To tell it I have referred to contemporary newspapers, to the *Supplementary History of Hartlepool* (attributed by Robert Wood to Thomas Wood), to Robert Martin's *Historical Notes of West Hartlepool and its Founder*, to Tomlinson's *North Eastern Railway*, to Robert Wood's *West Hartlepool*, and to correspondence, pamphlets and circulars published by Ralph Ward Jackson and by Benjamin Coleman.

I am also indebted to the Department of Palaeography and Diplomatic of the University of Durham, Durham County Council's Archivist, the Records Officer of the Church Commissioners, the British Library, the Public Record Office, Miss M. Hoban (Reference Librarian of Hartlepool Central Library), Mr. H. S. Middleton (Curator of Hartlepool Museums and Art Gallery) and the Rev. Christopher Bryant (Rector of Devizes), for information and copies of documents.

By the courtesy of Mr. N. D. Abram, Chief Executive of Hartlepool Borough Council, I have had access to the records of that Council and I am much indebted to my son-in-law, John Major, for his help in my research.

Some may feel that it would have been better not to have resurrected some of the details of the scandals which surrounded the early days of Christ Church, West Hartlepool, and to have left in obscurity the strange and sad record of Ralph Ward Jackson's downfall as the uncrowned king of the town of West

Hartlepool. But it is nearly one hundred years since he died and, surely, his achievements were great enough to stand the light of truth.

ERIC WAGGOTT
November, 1978.

Acknowledgments

The photograph of Ralph Ward Jackson (the *frontispiece*) is a copy of the *frontispiece* in Robert Martin's *Historical Notes of West Hartlepool and its Founder*; the photograph of Normanby Hall was taken for Hartlepool Borough Council in 1980, by courtesy of Mr. Charles Amer, and that Council have also provided the illustrations 3, 7, 8, 14 and 15 and the maps of West Hartlepool Docks and Town (illustrations 9 and 10). The drawing of the Atheneum as it was originally built is copied from the Supplement to Sharp's *History of Hartlepool* and the other photographs were taken by the author.

Jackson's Town

There is a Tide in the affairs of Men,
Which, taken at the flood, leads on to Fortune,
Omitted, all the voyage of their life
Is bound in shallows and in miseries.

Marcus Brutus in Shakespeare's
Julius Caesar.

This rather worrying thought may be as true of the affairs of towns as it is of those of the men and women who live in them. But perhaps it is not necessarily true. It may be that a man can sail his ship when the current is spent and yet beat his competitors who started before him and had the benefit of the flood water.

The tides in the affairs of the town which is now known only as "Hartlepool" can be counted on the fingers of two hands. Most of them were set going by the decision of one man, or of a small group of men. One that was not was the tide which flowed along the north-east coast of England during the first half of the nineteenth century and established that coast as the supreme coal-exporting seaboard of the world. It was the industrial revolution and, particularly, the invention of the steam engine and of railways. Some towns had taken it at the flood – the Tyne towns, Sunderland and Stockton. Middlesbrough and Seaham Harbour were late catching it. Hartlepool nearly missed it altogether, but just managed to embark on it as it was ebbing and, at the eleventh hour, became transformed from a small fishing port and summer holiday resort into a coal port. That change led, in time, to the creation of an industrial town of some consequence.

The credit, if credit it be, for initiating the scheme which, between 1832 and 1835, made the ancient natural harbour of Hartlepool a place suitable for the shipment of coal and connected it by twenty-three miles of railway to a few collieries in mid-Durham, must go to Christopher Tennant, a native of Yarm but then living in Hartlepool, and to Rowland Burdon of Castle Eden. But the creation and early development of the large industrial town which was founded on the existence of the coal port was the work of Ralph Ward Jackson. The way that he did it and the manner of man he was is as interesting a story as any that may be told about the many men whose imaginations were fired by the industrial revolution and who saw in it the hope of achieving great things for themselves and, sometimes, for others as well.

He had a dream of greatness – greatness for a port and town which he could call his own. It led him to commit reckless irregularities and, in the reckoning, he lost his position as king of the town which he had created. But the unique quality of towns is that, once they have grown to a substantial size, they do not disappear, even if, like Hiroshima, they are completely flattened. They are the nearest to being immortal of anything that man creates. And so, although Jackson ceased to be king, his creation lived on and continued to grow and prosper. Notwithstanding his calling it "West Hartlepool" and wishing it to be a separate port and town which he could rule as his own, it was really an addition to the ancient port and town of Hartlepool, and its nearness to that town made it inevitable that the two should, ultimately, be one.

Ralph Ward Jackson was born on the 7th of June, 1806, into a well-to-do middle class family who had been living at Normanby Hall since 1748. Normanby was then completely rural in character but would before long become a suburb of the new iron smelting and steel manufacturing town of Middlesbrough. He was the third of nine children, all born within a period of thirteen years to a mother who came from Berkshire and who would live for nearly forty-six years after bearing the last of them. Eight of them were boys and one, Ralph's next elder brother, William, was a clergyman who succeeded to Normanby Hall and lived there until his death in 1874. Ralph's next younger brother was Edwin about whom more will be heard in this story.

All the children had the second name of "Ward" but this was not hyphenated with "Jackson" at that time. It had also been given to their father and uncle, but not to their aunt. It seems to have been adopted by the family in memory and perpetuation of the name of their ancestress Hannah Ward, who had married Ralph's great-grandfather, George Jackson, in 1695. By the time of Ralph's death some writers were hyphenating the names but Ralph himself seems never to have done this.

After education at Rugby School he served Articles to a solicitor in Preston (Lancashire) and, after qualifying, practised at Stockton-on-Tees. There he became interested, mainly, in industrial and commercial undertakings, which included the Stockton and Hartlepool Railway Company. This had been formed in 1836 to make a line of eight miles to connect the Clarence Railway to the port of Hartlepool and, thus, to make Hartlepool, instead of the Tees, the terminal point for the shipment of coal from collieries in South-West Durham. Such a project was unpalatable to other ports and railways and, if it were to succeed, required rather unorthodox procedures. Jackson was just the man for that sort of thing and he related with pride how he had managed to get the leases and wayleaves without possessing compulsory powers. It is as straight a line as one is likely to find and an enduring testimony to his determination and persuasive ability. Of course he had to pay rather heavily for the rights, but he claimed, probably with justification, that if he had not done it that way it would never have been done at all.

Although he took the credit for getting the Clarence Railway to old Hartlepool, he was not the originator of the project. Christopher Tennant was the man who thought of it first, and the people of the ancient borough rightly regarded him as their friend and benefactor. Tennant had moved from Stockton to Hartlepool in about 1830, and he stayed there until he died in 1839, whilst on a visit to Leeds to try to arrange for the supply of fish from Hartlepool for the markets of West Yorkshire. He is buried in St. Hilda's Churchyard.

Jackson, on the other hand, seems never to have taken any real interest in old Hartlepool. Soon after his marriage in 1829 he made his home at Greatham Hall, some four and a half miles (as the crow flies) to the south-west of the borough but, at that time, without any rail, and only difficult and circuitous, road connection.

The reasons that led the Stockton and Hartlepool Railway Company to accept Hartlepool as their terminal port for the brief period of three years, and the alleged dispute between them and the Hartlepool Dock and Railway Company about the use of that port, are described in some detail in Martin's *Historical Notes of West Hartlepool* and Robert Wood's *West Hartlepool*. It seems probable, however, that, at least from the time that Jackson was in control of the Stockton and Hartlepool Company, it was his aim and intention to have his own port. Indeed, it could be put as harshly as that the Stockton and Hartlepool Company had only used the facilities of the Hartlepool Dock and Railway Company at old Hartlepool for the purpose of gaining a foothold in the Hartlepool Bay and, no doubt, many of the old Hartlepudlians saw it that way. For they did not like Jackson and many of them never got over their antipathy to him and his creation. From that stemmed the long feud between Hartlepool and West Hartlepool which gave rise to the ridiculous legend of the hanging of the monkey and which took more than a hundred and twenty years to be buried – it still makes occasional ghostly noises.

Although Jackson did not become Chairman of the Stockton and Hartlepool Railway Company until 1849 it seems probable that he was its dominating influence after the death of Christopher Tennant. He was also the guiding hand in the formation and incorporation of the Hartlepool West Harbour and Dock Company, which obtained its authority from Parliament to construct the West Harbour and Dock on the 23rd of May, 1844. He was then in a position to pursue his dream, the grandeur of which he revealed many years later when he was giving evidence to support the first application for a Charter of Incorporation for West Hartlepool, and was asked by the Chairman of the Improvement Commissioners:

I believe your idea originally was that West Hartlepool would ultimately become a port of Liverpool on the East Coast?

Jackson replied:

I always thought so, and that is my opinion still.

The site he had chosen for the building of his harbour was on the southern shore of the great tidal basin, known as the Slake, which lay between old Hartlepool, on the north-east, and Stranton, on the south-west. The seaside village of Seaton Carew was two miles away to the south. The population of the ancient borough was about 6,000, that of Stranton about 350 and that of Seaton Carew about the same.

Jackson was fond of describing his site as consisting of "sand-banks, mossy swamps and agricultural fields". He reminisced that when, in January, 1845, the first sod of his coal dock was cut at the back of some sand-hills, he amused himself by chasing a rabbit about the place "with very great delight".

The stone which was used to build the earliest buildings in West Hartlepool, including the Atheneum and Christ Church, came from excavations for the Coal Dock and the Jackson Dock and also from a quarry on the west side of what is now known as Clarence Road which later became the site of the Water Company's pumping station.

In 1844 it was not practicable to build a large harbour and dock without making provision for those who would construct and operate it. What is now called "commuting" was impossible for the working man and difficult for the wealthy. So Jackson would have had to build some houses and shops for his workmen, even if he had not wanted to do more than create a coal port. It is true that old Hartlepool had been much enlarged by its own harbour development but there was no great surplus of labour available there. Many of the navvies who had poured into Hartlepool to build the railway and harbour of the Hartlepool Dock and Railway Company had, by 1844, moved to other parts of the country.

> In eighteen hundred and forty-one
> Me corduroy britches I put on
> To work upon the railway, the railway, the railway.
> In eighteen hundred and forty-two
> From Hartlepool I moved to Crewe
> And found meself a job to do
> Working on the railway, the railway, the railway,
> Poor Paddy works on the railway.

So goes the traditional Irish ballad recorded by "The Dubliners", and as they sing it they are reciting history.

Five years earlier the minutes of the Hartlepool Literary, Scientific and Mechanical Institution had recorded that "nearly all the Mechanics having left the town in consequence of the stoppage of the public works, the few members that remain in the Institution deem its continuance useless under such circumstances". The stoppage referred to was the completion of the original Hartlepool railway and dock, from which, on the 9th of July, 1835, Cuthbert Sharp's brig *The Britannia*, had sailed with the first cargo of coal ever shipped from Hartlepool. There was no welfare state, not even a "dole", in those days.

So Jackson had to plan a town, as well as a harbour and dock. Perhaps a village would have sufficed if he had had nothing more in his mind than the construction and servicing of a coal port. But he had much more in mind. The town he intended to build would be not only a coal port but a general cargo port with sufficient industry and commerce to maintain a flow of traffic – imports as well as exports – which were essential to make such a port great and prosperous. And it must be a fine place – well-planned and with the amenities expected of a new town in the mid-nineteenth century.

Having provided the first houses in what soon became

known as "California", (the area adjoining the west end of Hart Road Cemetery), in Harbour Terrace, in "Old Town" and in Throston Street (now called Rium Terrace), he set about his main task and planned a splendid wide street, to be known as Church Street, with other streets running into it at right angles on its south side. And in Church Street there would be public buildings of character and dignity.

The first of these was the Atheneum. It was commenced in 1851, four years after the West Harbour had opened, and it was finished in less than a year. The site was given by Jackson's Company and they also gave the stone of which it was made. Jackson made a personal contribution of £100 to its cost, which totalled £1,100. The building originally consisted of:

Basement floor: A school-room, kitchen, laboratory and store-room.
Ground floor: A news-room, library, two class-rooms and two rooms for a caretaker.
First floor: A large lecture-room, with retiring-room and offices.

It was designed by the land-agent of the dock company and built by him and other employees of the company. At first it was used mainly for the activities of the West Hartlepool Literary and Mechanics Institution, but when the West Hartlepool Improvement Commissioners came into existence, in 1854, it was used also as a town hall. The Commissioners (of whom Jackson was chairman) had their meetings in the large lecture-room and it was there that Jackson's full-length portrait by Francis Grant was hung when it was presented to the Commissioners on the 23rd of October, 1855. Also, in a single room in the Atheneum all the business of the Commissioners was carried on until shortly before the Municipal Buildings were opened in 1889.

The total harbour and dock development achieved by Jackson, during his reign of less than twenty years, was the

West Harbour (44 acres), the Coal Dock (8 acres), the Jackson Dock (13 acres) and the Swainson and Timber Dock (13 acres). He also constructed a timber pond and two graving docks. This harbour and dock system was completely separate from the harbour and docks of old Hartlepool. There was no rail connection (Jackson severed that which had previously existed) and only rudimentary road connection.

His total town development was described by Robert Martin, remembering it as it was when he was eight years old, in 1862, as consisting "approximately" of the following property:

> All New Stranton (now the Old Town), Harbour, Victoria, Commercial and Albert Terraces, nearly all Church Street, Edward Street, odd buildings in Mainsforth Terrace, part of George Street, John Street, part of Princess Street, Dover Street, Jersey Street, Exeter Street, Hope Street, part of Upper Surtees Street, the south side of Upper Reed Street, Mosley Street, Freeman Street, part of Lamb Street, Catherine Street, Thomas Street, Ramsey Street, James Street, Hilda Street, Pilgrim Street, a few buildings in Musgrave Street (then Stranton Lane), part of Whitby Street, part of Tower Street, one side of Park Street, Queen Street, all the "A" Streets from Anson Street to Andrew Street, Tower Terrace, Robinson Street, William Street, Brown Street, Harrison Street, St. James' Place, Regents Place, Carlisle Place, nearly the whole of Stockton Street to Musgrave Street, Burn Terrace, Brunton Street and Bower Street". "This", he said, "to our recollection, was West Hartlepool, with a population of about 12,000. Very few buildings, except farm buildings, existed to the west of Stockton Street or the north of Fountain Terrace".

Most of these streets have now disappeared and the Swainson Dock has been filled in. Where they lay can be seen on the map on page 134 and on old street maps (one or two have been reproduced in Robert Wood's *West Hartlepool*), and a very good impression of what the harbour and town looked like as Jackson's reign was coming to an end can be gained from the two beautiful paintings by J. W. Carmichael which are in the possession of the Hartlepool Borough Council.

All ports must have some industry to serve them and the ships which use them. When old Hartlepool became a coal port in 1835 it soon attracted some of that kind of industry. Thomas Richardson, who had a foundry at Castle Eden, came there and, in partnership with John Parkin of Sunderland, built the first ship in the new coal port and appropriately named it *The Castle Eden*. He moved over to adjacent Middleton in 1838 and thus the origin of the great marine engineering industry of Richardson-Westgarth's was established. There were four other shipbuilders in Middleton – one of the firms, J. P. Denton & Co., overshadowing the others in output and being the forerunner of the Hartlepools' greatest industry from 1866 to 1962 – William Gray & Co. Ltd.

But old Hartlepool was still deficient in port industries and commerce. As Thomas Wood said in 1851 – "There is still much to be done before Hartlepool can be looked upon as complete in itself." He also wrote of the five shipping firms – the Original, the General, the Union, the Commercial, and the Phoenix – which had started up in Hartlepool between 1835 and 1843, but had all failed before 1847.

So Jackson was faced with daunting tasks if he was to move towards the realisation of his dream for the new port and town.

The first was to secure a greatly increased coal export. This was difficult enough. There were too many coal ports on the thirty miles of coast from the Tyne to the Tees and the West Dock, being the last of them, had to get coal, either by taking trade from one or more of the others, or by getting new collieries connected to the port.

The second task was to attract new commerce to the port and to build up a general cargo traffic. To pave the way for this, Jackson built two large warehouses with stone from his quarries – one facing the Jackson Dock and the other adjoining the Swainson Dock.

How the Trade was Won

Jackson's greatest asset was his unbelievable energy. He

did not wait for things to happen – he made them happen.

The proprietors of the Hartlepool Railway and Dock Company had been very disappointed by the poor return which they had obtained from the spending of what, in those days, was regarded as a large sum of money to improve the Hartlepool Harbour and to complete the Victoria Dock in order to take the promised 318,000 tons of coal a year from the Clarence Railway's connection to their coal drops. They had, over three years, had a total of only 115,000 tons, i.e. an average of 38,300 tons a year.

From the moment that the West Dock opened the Clarence coal traffic, now largely diverted to that dock, increased miraculously. In 1848, 169,000 tons; in 1849, 389,000 tons; in 1850, 590,000 tons. How had this been achieved? Partly no doubt, by a greater diversion of the Port Clarence coal traffic to the West Dock, partly by a general increase in the production of coal, partly by the sinking of new pits on the lines connected to the dock, but mainly by Jackson's having acquired interests in a considerable number of collieries which had, as a result, become tied to his dock. To acquire those interests he had used money which was not his own and which his company had no legal right to use for that purpose. By so doing he gave lethal ammunition to his enemies which, in later years, they would use against him.

He also busied himself in trying to persuade shipowners, industrialists and men of commerce to come to his town and trade through his docks. He soon had a shipbuilder, John Pile, building ships on the piece of land which lay between the Jackson Dock and the Swainson Dock – later to be known as Gray's Old Yard. He also attracted a sea captain, Robert Irvine, who became marine superintendent to his company and later established a shipyard launching into the harbour.

There had been an iron foundry in Old Town, run by Samuel Bastow, but he moved into Mainsforth Terrace (Cliff House) when the West Dock was opened. Before long there were three iron foundries in the middle of the rapidly growing town – two in Hope Street and one in Whitby Street. Also there were a few blacksmiths shops adjacent to the Coal Dock. All the houses in the town burned coal. In winter the sky was filled with dirt.

Other industries necessary for the operation of the port quickly appeared – a sailmaker in Old Town, a mast and block maker in the dock area. However, the most pressing need was to get shipowners to use the port. As previously mentioned the first attempts to establish shipowning in old Hartlepool had failed. But, by 1860, 194 ships were registered at the port and, of these, 13 were registered in the part ownership of Ralph Ward Jackson. He had acquired these vessels for the purpose of building up the trade of his harbour and docks and for encouraging the use of the port by other shipowners. Soon he had established regular cargo and passenger services to St. Petersburg, Hamburg and Rotterdam. Not only was coal leaving the port in increasing quantities but general cargo was coming in and the large warehouses were being used. A vigorous attempt was being made to build up an import of livestock. Much more significantly, as it eventually turned out, timber was becoming an important element in the port's trade. In 1861, 2,042,128 tons of coal and coke and 61,496 tons of general goods were exported and 204,724 tons of grain, 33,529 tons of general goods and 59,250 tons of timber were imported.*

Jackson's ships had been acquired by irregular means, similar to those used to obtain the collieries. Trouble lay ahead because of these transactions but, for the moment, he had given the impression of a booming new port and other shipowners quickly came to share in the prosperity, some from abroad or elsewhere in the neighbourhood, some from within the town itself, because, in those days, shipowning did not require the wealth of a magnate or of a great company. A few shares in a ship could be bought for what would now be considered a very modest sum – much less than the cost of a modern house.

*These figures are for the Port of Hartlepool, which for Customs purposes comprised old Hartlepool and West Hartlepool.

Of great significance among the new town's shipowners was one whose name was to become world-famous. Robert Ropner, an immigrant from Prussia, started business in West Hartlepool in partnership with Thomas Appleby. Many others were operating by 1862 and, ten years earlier, Christopher Furness had been born in Old Town. He would be a grocer in Lynn Street before he developed a shipping business which became one of the largest in the world.

The foundations laid by Jackson were destined to make the Port of Hartlepool, in its heyday, fourth in the United Kingdom for registered shipping tonnage and the largest timber importing port on the north-east coast.

Hull and Grimsby had most of the timber trade when Jackson came to power and he decided that he must get some of it. In 1852 there had been only one timber firm regularly using the West Dock, but soon several more had been persuaded by Jackson to come to his town or, at least, to open a branch there. His arch-enemy of the future, Benjamin Coleman, alleged that he induced them to come by reckless offers. In his circular of the 12th of July, 1860, addressed to the share and debenture holders of Jackson's Company he said this:

> The leading merchants of the ports of Hull and Great Grimsby have personally assured me that it is impossible to conceive anything more reckless than the course pursued by Mr. Jackson in his endeavours to secure the foreign trade, which is chiefly in grain and timber. The "conspirators", as Mr. Jackson will, no doubt, call them, say that from first to last he has carried on the trade connected with the West Hartlepool docks and steamboats at a great loss, and I have little doubt you will find that a large item of the admitted unauthorised additional outlay of a million of your capital has been sunk in his endeavours to supplant the Hull and Great Grimsby merchants.
>
> I will give you some instances – the ordinary rates for freight, from Rotterdam *to Great Grimsby*, for grain, is 2s. to 2s. 6d. per quarter. Mr. Jackson took grain for a through-rate, from Rotterdam to Burton-on-Trent, at 2s. 8d. per quarter; which, after paying

charges and dues to other interests, left him just *five pence* per quarter for the use of his boats, docks and railway.

An old-established firm at Hull, with timber trade, found such advantages were offered for conducting their trade at West Hartlepool, the company [*meaning Jackson's Company*] doing all the agency business, paying duties, &c., &c., without making a charge for it, were induced for self-protection, to open a branch business at West Hartlepool; and, on one occasion, immediately after the reduction of the timber duties, they were about to remove a cargo of timber and deals out of bond, when they found, instead of paying 1s. per load, which was the amount of the reduced duty, they were asked to pay 7s. 6d. per load, which was the amount of the old duty, the West Hartlepool Company having in their excessive zeal and obliging practice, paid the duty of 7s. 6d. long before the reduction took place.

Of course, the firm not having given orders to pay the higher duty, refused to pay more than the existing duty of 1s. per load, and the West Hartlepool Company, consequently, had to sustain the loss of 6s. 6d. per load, and the loss of interest for the long period they had so unnecessarily paid the duty by anticipation. This mode of doing business appears very wild and meaningless, but there is still a "method in his madness", which does not meet the eye at first, and it is this – Mr. Jackson has the practice, as you must have seen on all occasions, of parading large figures as a proof "of the growing importance and rising prosperity of the youngest port in the Kingdom", and by showing at a particular period, say just before his annual statement, that the trade of the last *two* months had increased by a certain amount over the same period last year, he would probably make his calculations for the remaining 10 months of the year on the basis of the two, which have no doubt been forced by some such operation as this timber transaction, and thus his statement on this head becomes one among his many delusive misleadings.

Whether or not Coleman's allegations were true, Jackson's enterprise did succeed as far as the timber trade was concerned. The incoming merchants found the port ideal and the 60,000, or so, tons of timber coming into the port at the end of Jackson's reign would be multiplied eight or nine times in some years that lay ahead. The timber and forest products trade is now the main reason for the port's existence.

Moreover, although the first shipyard that Jackson had induced to start in the West Dock (Pile Spence & Company's) failed in 1866, it was taken over, three years later, by the Middleton firm of Denton, Gray & Co. William Gray had come to old Hartlepool in 1843 and had opened a draper's shop in Church Street, West Hartlepool, by 1852. Now he was to play the major part, in the second half of the nineteenth century, in developing the town which Jackson had founded into a successful industrial community. It has been said that, as the statue of Ralph Ward Jackson looks eastward down Church Street at the town which he built, so the statue of William Gray looks westward from the other end of Christ Church at the town that he built. Certainly to him, his sons and to that other giant of the maritime world, Christopher Furness, Hartlepool owes much of the industry that supported it for one hundred years and which still contributes substantially to its economy.

William Gray developed the most productive shipyard in the country. He established a major marine engineering business. His son, Matthew, was mainly responsible for keeping the iron and steel industry in existence in West Hartlepool until 1896, and later the Gray family sustained it in the face of a threatened take-over.

The Grays and Christopher Furness were instrumental in promoting such industries as The Expanded Metal Company and the Greatham Salt Works. If Gray's had not built the graving dock at Graythorpe, Laing's Offshore would never have been there. Often one thing leads to another but it is to him who initiates the change that the credit, or blame, must primarily go and, undoubtedly, Ralph Ward Jackson changed Hartlepool from a coal port into being, in addition, a timber port and an industrial town.

It is sad that of the many businesses that came to West Hartlepool between 1847 and 1862, few now remain there. The West Hartlepool Steam Navigation Company Ltd. are, in a sense, the direct descendants of Ralph Ward Jackson, for it was in their name that he ran the regular services to Hamburg and St. Petersburg in 1856, and it was in their name that the steamboats continued to operate when Jackson was dethroned. The sawmills of Robert Lauder & Co. Ltd. were founded by Robert Lauder in 1853 and they still carry on their business in the same place with a Robert Lauder in charge. The largest of the Jackson era industries now surviving in Hartlepool is the Lion Brewery, founded by William Waldon in 1852, but later taken over by John William Cameron and now one of the major breweries of the north of England.

Jackson's Church

As the Atheneum was being built in 1851, Jackson was, among many other things, thinking about the spiritual welfare of his people. He had engaged a London architect, E. B. Lamb, to design a fine church to stand at the head of the wide avenue that led to the docks and on the south side of which the grid-iron pattern of streets was rapidly filling with houses, offices, warehouses, and factories.

If proof were needed that Jackson was not a mere speculator, trying to make the most money for himself in the shortest possible time, the fact that he built a large church to fulfil what he saw as one of the first needs of his new creation must surely provide that proof. No money was to be made out of a church and there was already an ancient church at Stranton which could be regarded as meeting the needs of the Anglicans. True, it was far too small for the growing community, but it was the Parish Church, embracing the new town, and, if it needed enlargement or duplication, the Church authorities might have been left to see to it.

However Jackson, or more correctly his Company, gave the site and the stone to build a large church which was to be known as Christ Church and which would eventually have a district of its own. It was started in April, 1852 and finished in April, 1854. In modern terms it cost an unbelievably small sum of money. Martin says £6,000 plus £400 for the bells, but a circular published by Jackson at the time of the consecration said that the amount then subscribed was about £2,000 and a further £1,500 was needed. In the same circular Jackson's personal donation was shown as £200. The largest single money contribution came from Mrs. Surtees of Mainsforth, who gave £1,000 to provide the endowment fund. In a letter, written in April, 1856, Jackson said that the cost was double the estimate and, "out of £8,000 expenditure, £7,800 and upwards has been provided by my own relatives, friends and myself". What the true cost was we shall never know, because detailed accounts were not kept and, as was often the case with Jackson, it is difficult to distinguish between what he owned, or paid out of his own pocket, and what was owned or contributed by his Company. And what was the value of the site and the stone?

The church is remarkable in form. A relatively huge tower gives the impression of a nave and chancel much larger than they are. The finials seem to suggest that they might be crosses but are not sure about it. Incongruously attached to the finial on the gable of the south transept is a large stone anchor. The little spire which sprouts from the top of the tower must surely have been intended, not only to point the way to Heaven, but also to guide the mariner into Jackson's harbour. Generally the shapes are strange and rather outrageous, but the total result is interesting if not beautiful. Like its founder, it is bold and, perhaps, a trifle big in the head! There is no foundation stone but the architect seems to have left his signature in a small carving protruding from the lower part of the south side of the tower.

As the church neared completion Jackson's mind turned to the legal and administrative arrangements that would be necessary to enable it to function as an Anglican Church. As it was a "subscription" church he adopted the usual procedure of appointing trustees to manage the trust fund that was to constitute the endowment and to exercise the right of patronage – i.e. of nominating Incumbents. The five trustees he selected were: himself, his father-in-law (Charles Swainson), his brother-in-law (the Rev. Henry Walter McGrath), the Vicar of Seaton Carew (the Rev. John Lawson) and a Durham clergyman (the Rev. George Townsend Fox). Charles Swainson was very old and lived near Preston (Lancashire). As Jackson himself said, he "never did wish to be involved in a trust of this sort". The Rev. McGrath was, he said, "by

no means well" and "was in Italy for the benefit of his health
and had a hesitation at first to be named in the documents".
Hardly suitable people for the job in hand, one might think,
but one must remember that it was really Jackson's church.
He would make the decisions and the others would not be
expected to do more than give the occasional assenting nod.

Although there must have been some informal agreement
with the Vicar of Stranton and his Patron before the church
was started, Jackson left the formal administrative and legal
arrangements until only a few months before the building was
completed. Then, through his London agents, Bell, Steward
and Lloyd, he instructed a barrister to prepare the necessary
documents. They were:

> The trust deed for the endowment and the exercise of the
> patronage.
> A Declaration by the Bishop of Durham assigning a district
> to the church.
> A Declaration by the Bishop vesting the patronage in the
> five trustees.
> Two licences by the Bishop to authorise the incumbent to
> solemnize marriages and to administer the sacraments or
> services of Churchings and Baptisms in the church.

They were submitted to the Bishop, Edward Maltby, through
his legal adviser, the Deputy Registrar of the Diocese (Joseph
Davison, a Durham solicitor), and the Bishop accepted them
and complied with them. A district was assigned (carved out
of the Parish of Stranton) and the licences were issued.

About the same time as he had the documents prepared,
Jackson, with the assent of his co-trustees, chose the man
whom he would nominate for the incumbency. He was a curate
at Norton, near Stockton-on-Tees, named John Hart Burges.
He was twenty-eight years old and had been ordained about
four years previously. After serving as a curate at St. Stephen's,
South Shields, he had come to Norton in 1852. No doubt when
he heard that he was to become a curate in West Hartlepool

and, when Christ Church was completed, the first incumbent of this fine new church in this expanding new town, he would have been pleased. The income he would receive (about £230 per annum) was not very large but, by the standards of those days, it would be adequate and twice what he was getting at Norton. There was no parsonage as yet but one was about to be built in Church Square and in the meantime he would be given a rent-free house in Albert Terrace (the first section of Mainsforth Terrace).

He came to West Hartlepool early in 1854 and immediately worked assiduously to get to know his people.

On the 20th of April, 1854, Bishop Maltby consecrated the church and services commenced. Robert Martin records that he was born on the day of the consecration and was the twelfth child Christened in the church, so it must have been quite busy from the start.

A letter published in the *Durham Chronicle* in 1856 and signed "Fiat Justitia", said:

During the year 1854, everything went on agreeably – the clergyman was zealous and active, and Mr. Jackson, his patron and friend, liberally and fairly supported him. In the winter of that year the cholera broke out in West Hartlepool, and the kind and courageous Ministrations of the reverend incumbent gained him golden opinions.

But storm clouds were gathering over the relationship between Jackson and the curate.

Ostensibly they were caused by one matter of great importance to both men. That was the schools which Jackson had planned to have built as the third item of his provision for the welfare of his people.

The only day school in the Parish of Stranton (other than a few small private schools in dwellinghouses) was the New Fulthorpe School, which had been built in 1841 on a site near to that now occupied by the Co-op Central Stores. It had one room and, if packed, could accommodate about forty boys of the old village of Stranton. In 1854 there were some 6,000

inhabitants in the parish, which now embraced West Hartlepool, and the need for large public schools for both sexes was
urgent.

Before Burges had taken up his appointment, Jackson had
discussed with him the question of the schools and had made
it clear that he would rely on him to raise the funds that would
be needed and generally to oversee the project, but that
Jackson's Company would give the site and the stone to build
them.

Burges set about the task enthusiastically and prepared a
Memorial for submission to the Education Committee of the
Privy Council, asking for a grant. It was signed by Jackson,
his son and other prominent townsmen and, if it had been
read carefully, it would have raised the question of the area
which the schools were intended to serve. It left no doubt that
they were to be "National" schools (i.e. Church of England
Schools) "intended for the instruction of the children of the
labouring Poor". But Jackson was exceedingly busy with other
matters and perhaps he did not read it carefully.

Burges had no doubt that the schools were to be Church
schools serving the district to be assigned to his church and,
that being so, the children of that district would have priority
over the children in the remainder of the parish of Stranton,
and Anglicans would have priority over Nonconformists. In
Jackson's mind, however, whilst they would be Church of
England schools, they would be available to all the poor
children of his new town, regardless of their residence in or
out of the district of Christ Church and regardless of whether
they were, or were not, Anglicans. Although Burges never said
so, and would probably have denied it, the importance of the
attachment of the schools to Christ Church involved more than
the allocation of the accommodation available – it concerned
the shade of doctrine to be taught and, above all, the question
of who was to be in charge of the day-to-day management
of the schools.

This difference of view did not become apparent until the
project had progressed some way and Burges had collected

£334 and had also been promised a grant of nearly £2,000 from the Government.

It may be, however, that there was more to cause friction between the two men than the schools affair. Fiat Justitia's letter to the *Durham Chronicle* had also said this:

> During the early and middle parts of the year 1855 all seemed well, though after events would lead a close observer to suspect that the increasing popularity of Mr. Burges had given umbrage to his powerful friend – though that popularity had never been sought by Mr. Burges, but was, among a grateful people, the natural result of untiring energy and works of love in his ministry among them.

Who was Fiat Justitia? Not Burges himself but, it would seem, his legal adviser, William Blanchard, of Leeds.

The dispute about the schools was first revealed at a meeting of the schools' committee in Christ Church vestry on Saturday, the 17th of November, 1855. The committee comprised Jackson, his son, Ralph Walker, William Thompson, Edward Turnbull and Burges (who described himself as "chairman" to the annoyance of Jackson). Jackson not only made it clear that the schools must be available to the children of the whole of the town but indulged in a personal attack on Burges, in which wounding things were said which had nothing to do with the schools' question.

Burges was upset and, on the following Monday, twice tried to see Jackson, but without success. So, on the evening of that day he wrote a long and revealing letter in which he referred to the grievances which he thought his patron was holding against him and which arose out of a great banquet which had been held on Tuesday, the 23rd of October, in the Atheneum.

The banquet had been organised to celebrate the handing over to Jackson of his full-length portrait "by the inhabitants of West Hartlepool and other persons who have subscribed for the painting of the same". The presentation was made by George Leeman, who was not one of the inhabitants, but a

York man. How many of the inhabitants had subscribed is anybody's guess, but, possibly, not many. Leeman said the subscribers were "scattered all over the country." A few years earlier the same inhabitants were supposed to have subscribed for an enormous silver centre-piece which had been presented to Jackson just in time for it to be exhibited in the Great Exhibition of 1851. Perhaps one ought not to be so suspicious as to harbour the thought that these presentations might have been part of a publicity campaign for Jackson and his port and town. At all events, the portrait, which had been painted by Francis Grant R.A., at a cost of £339, was immediately handed back by Jackson to the recently-created Town Improvement Commissioners, on permanent loan, and on condition that it should be hung in the lecture-room of the Atheneum until the town had a town hall. It was transferred to the Council Chamber of the Municipal Buildings in 1889 and there it stayed until the end of the County Borough of West Hartlepool and, indeed, until the Municipal Buildings were vacated in 1976.

The presentation, and the dinner which followed it, had been organised as a great occasion by a committee under the chairmanship of William Hutton. *The Stockton and Hartlepool Mercury* said of it:

> The day was one which will ever be memorable in the history of West Hartlepool. From every ship in the docks, and from every available altitude, colours floated gaily in the breeze; the hum of business was suspended shortly after midday, when the shops were closed and the workmen in the place set free to enjoy themselves. The bells rang out a joyous peal, their music blending with unceasing boom of cannon, Strangers innumerable from distant places thronged the streets; and the town was one universal scene of holiday. And the occasion certainly justified this festal pomp; for perhaps in the whole history of our country's commerce no instance can be found to parallel the rise and progress of West Hartlepool – a town which a few years ago had not begun to exist; which is now a busy and populous commercial emporium bidding fair to outrival the largest ports of the United Kingdom. And when we remember that this result is the offspring of one man's genius,

energy, and perseverance – a man whose dauntless courage and enterprising spirit laughed at obstacles, which would have overwhelmed hundreds, and who has lived to see in the docks and harbour, the shipping with which they are crowded, the bustling quays, the populous streets, and its railway, and steamboats, and a host of adjuncts which ever distinguish a rising commercial port – who has lived to see in all this the triumph of his perseverance and determination – it is not to be wondered, we say, that the name of Ralph Ward Jackson, for he is the man who has accomplished this, should be honoured by the people of West Hartlepool; nor that they should seek to perpetuate his fame by handing down to posterity the lineaments of his form and features.

The actual presentation took place in the Atheneum at one o'clock. George Leeman was the deputy chairman of the North Eastern Railway Company, which company would soon take over the Hartlepool Dock and Railway Company and was, as Jackson said, already in possession of that undertaking.

He had been a close associate of Jackson's for twenty years and had worked with him to secure the passing of the Hartlepool Pier and Port Bill which had just become law and which authorised the construction of a huge "Harbour of Refuge" in Hartlepool Bay. He made a long speech praising Jackson and his success in building the port and trade of West Hartlepool. The portrait was accepted on permanent loan to the town by the Rev. H. R. Ridley, Vicar of Stranton and a member of the recently established Town Improvement Commissioners.

At six o'clock the Dinner commenced in the large hall of the Atheneum. The meal was provided by Mr. Murray of the Royal Hotel, "in a perfectly *recherché* style, the viands and the wine being equally commendable in quality". The principal guests were: George Leeman, Ralph Ward Jackson ("the guest of the evening"), Dr. De Vetre of Lancaster and Isaac Lowthian Bell, Mayor of Newcastle (who would, twenty years later, be elected Member of Parliament for the Hartlepools). About 200 male guests sat down to dinner, during which the West Hartlepool brass band played outside. The cannon continued to boom at intervals.

When the meal was over "a number of ladies – many of them in elegant dress costume – entered the room and gave an additional interest to the scene", and the toasts and speeches began. These were interspersed with solos, duets, and glees by "the gentlemen of the Durham choir". All the toasts were preceded by speeches, some very long, and many were followed by equally lengthy responses. Space will permit little more than a list of them:

Toast   "The Queen"
           Music – "God Save the Queen"

Toast   "Prince Albert and the rest of the royal family"
           Glee – "Hail Royal Heir of England"

Toast   "Our Allies, the Emperor of the French, the King of Sardinia, and the Sultan of Turkey"
           proposed by the Chairman (George Leeman)
(These allies were those of the British in the Crimean War, then in progress. Much opprobrium was heaped upon Russia, "who sought to lull the whole of Europe into fancied security, and then crush its liberty".)
        Song – "Sebastopol is Won" – Mr. Kaye.

Toast   "The Army and Navy"
            proposed by the Chairman
    Duet – "The Army and Navy" – Mr. Ashton and Mr. Hemingway.

Toast   "The Health of Ralph Ward Jackson, the Founder of the Port and Town of West Hartlepool"
proposed by the Chairman and "to be drunk with bumpers"
      Song – "I'd rather be an Englishman" –
               Mr. Hemingway
("sung in his very best style and rapturously applauded")
Response by Ralph Ward Jackson, ("received with a burst of applause which lasted for some minutes, the effect being heightened by the waving of handkerchiefs from the ladies . . . and the reiterated boom

of the cannon outside"). For part of Jackson's speech, see his Obituary in the Appendix, but, in addition to what is reported there, he made long reference to the desirability of building the harbour of refuge, and suggested that, to overcome the problem of its great cost, convict labour should be used in preference to spending money in sending the convicts out to foreign lands.

By this time things had become too much for the Mayor of Newcastle, and he had left the room "in consequence of indisposition". He should have proposed the next toast, but his duties were carried out by the already much overworked Chairman, who proposed:

Toast   "The Town and Trade of West Hartlepool"

This was followed by another glee and another response by Jackson, during which he was moved, apparently without premeditation, to seek to calm any feelings of jealousy or resentment on the part of old Hartlepool by proposing:

Toast   "Success to the Town and Trade of Old Hartlepool, coupled with the name of Mr. Jobson"

Mr. E. S. Jobson said he "felt at a loss to express himself, as Mr. Jackson had certainly taken him by surprise". He did the best he could in the circumstances and raised some laughter by saying that "West Hartlepool had, to a certain extent, brought the old Hartlepool people out'. The toasts were now tending to proliferate and the Chairman had another go:

Toast   "Success to the Harbour of Refuge"
Glee – "Spring's Delight"
Response by Edward Turnbull

Toast   "The Health of the Chairman"
proposed by Jackson
Glee – "Since First I Saw Thy Face"
Response by George Leeman, during which he

proposed:

Toast   "The Health of Mr. William Charles Ward
Jackson, the son of the distinguished guest"
(Leeman seized the occasion to designate William
Charles as Ralph's successor when he should retire,
for "with all the bloom that settles itself on the cheek
of my friend on the right, almost like a peach
blossom, the time will come when he must give
way".)

Glee – "Deep in a Flowery Vale"

Response by Wm. Charles Ward Jackson, who
spoke of his father with admiration and devotion

Toast   "Success to the West Hartlepool Harbour and
Railway Company"
proposed by Mr. W. Clunie
Glee – "See our Oars"

Response by Dr. De Vetre, "who replied at very
considerable length", and took the opportunity of
proposing:

Toast   "The Coal and Iron Trade of the District"

Response by Mr. John Robson of the City of
Durham (who spoke "in courteous terms of great
brevity").

Toast   "The North Eastern Railway Company"
proposed by Ralph Ward Jackson
Glee – "Foresters sound the Cheerful Horn"

Response by Mr. Sheriff, who said another toast
"has been put into my hand". It was:

Toast   "The Shipping Interest"
Response by Mr. John Pile

Toast   "The West Hartlepool Improvement
Commissioners"
proposed by the Chairman
Glee – "By Celia's Bower"
Response by Mr. William Ramsey
Glee – "Great Father Bacchus"

Toast   "The Portrait Committee"
                   proposed by the Chairman.
                   Response by Mr. William Hutton
Toast   "The Health of Mrs. Jackson"
                   proposed by the Chairman
Response by Ralph Ward Jackson, who said –
"Mrs. Jackson would have been present amongst
us, but she feared she could not have withstood the
emotion. As it is, however, her heart is with us."
(*Great Cheering!*)
Toast   "The Ladies"
                   proposed by Mr. W. C. W. Jackson
                   Response by Mr. Clunie

It was then a few minutes to midnight and "the assembly
separated, the proceedings having been characterized throughout by an unbroken spirit of harmony".

The Rev. Burges was at this gargantuan dinner but seems
not to have enjoyed himself. He left early, if 10.55 p.m. can
be called early, and he heard, or thought he heard, afterwards
that his patron was displeased with him for this and for other
things connected with the occasion. His letter of the 19th
November, starts:

Dear Mr. Jackson,
    As I have called twice today and could not see you, I think
it better to write. I have no doubt, if I could see you quietly, and
speak matters over, without the intervention of other parties, we
should both be able to see there must have been some mischief-
makers at work to break up the unanimity which hitherto has
subsisted between us. I am sure that all the little matters that have
reached my ears must have annoyed you, but I think it would
have been only just to me that you should have asked me whether
they were true without holding them against me in your conduct
to me, as I plainly saw was the case in your conversations with
me in your office some time since; and again in your language
and bearing to me at the vestry meeting on Saturday, and which
I assure you was not very pleasant or easy to endure, and I think
you will not feel was quite fair to me, as a Minister of the Gospel,

unable and unwilling to resent, and only anxious for the discharge of my duty.

I should not think of answering some of the things I have heard, only, I tell you plainly I have always been fond of you, and am therefore, sorry that anyone should have turned you against me in this manner. Now, with respect to the bells, so far from not wishing to have them rung at the presentation of your picture – several days before I told the bell-ringers they would have to ring all day on that day – Nelson immediately answered, Who is to pay us? I told him I was sure the committee would, but anyway, Nelson, "If no one else pays you, I will pay myself – and you can come up on the Monday evening to me or the church-wardens, and I will direct you what times to ring." Again, about the dinner, you know that I never go to anything of that kind, but not only did I go on that occasion but I paid for my brother, and went to beg of Mr. James and Mr. Fox to come likewise, – and as to remarks afterwards, the sum and substance of my remark was this:– "That of all your works they left out the best and the one most calculated to bring the blessing of God upon all the others – your care for their souls". What I said about the grace, I said to yourself, – "that I did not like to dine without asking a blessing." Then about leaving the room. About half-past ten – upon looking down the room, I saw my mother trying to open the window, and fearing she was getting one of her faintings upon her, I sent down (either your own servant or Mr. Brewster's) to ask her "would she wish to go out." She sent word she would not (it turned out afterwards it was Mrs. Ridley who was not well); and even then, I had heard all the parts of the proceedings I wished especially to hear – Mr. Leeman's, your own, and your son's speeches. Then at five minutes to eleven, my brother asked your son what time the train started, – he said he believed eleven, but called out to ask Mr. Chester, who confirmed it. My brother and I both got up at once and went away – my brother declaring that if the train was gone, he would walk all the way home, though he had not been in bed all the night before. When he arrived home, after the dinner, he found his wife had been confined in the meantime. Now I ask you, as a candid man, does this simple, truthful account agree with all the varnished tales you have been told, and fancied, and then caused you to act towards me in a manner I never could have expected, and calculated to do the cause of truth injury, – and not only this but to cause much ill-feeling in the town. I must also mention what I did not think you would have done, viz., – calling a meeting of one churchwarden, (*my* churchwarden, elected by me according to the power given me by the act (Wm. 4th.), under which this church is built, as I found in the book you sent me), and leaving out Mr. Crosby, the *people's* churchwarden, – and with him and a few others, informing the organist that he was *not* under my direction, and other things of the same kind. I think, therefore, it will be wise to have the Archdeacon down on the spot to arrange all these matters, if you think well of it. I expected you would have supported me instead of going against me.

And now about the schools. I am satisfied that when you think over it, you will not have them built for Stranton as well as this, but will agree with me, and with your own former wishes, – upon which I commenced and worked all through, – that they should only be in connection with this district ...

And he went on, elaborating his argument on the schools.

Jackson replied immediately (he usually did in all his correspondence, no matter how busy or fatigued he might be):

West Hartlepool, 20 Nov. 1855

Dear Mr. Burges,

I have just received your long note of yesterday's date and am surprised you should deem it necessary to lay any stress upon matters which you say are connected with the dinner on the 23rd Oct. – for which I really have nothing to do, of which I am almost entirely ignorant and to which I have obviously made no reference, nor ever intend that such trifles as you allude to in this respect shall have any effect on my mind in respect of the important points which are at present in agitation and connected with yourself. I never tittle tattle, nor am led in my judgment upon grave and interesting subjects by hearsays and reports, and I think it would have been more sensible and discreet if you were not so open and sensitive to them. You unfortunately also consider that, if a person does not actually agree with you in any matter which you deem it *your* duty to take up and promote, he comes a personal opponent and that antagonism necessarily must result towards you. I do not think you are liberal enough to concede to others the same

right and capability of judging what may be good and useful as
you claim for yourself.

And then, ominously:

> And I feel satisfied that an unbending disposition on your part
> in this respect is productive of disquietude and unpleasant feelings
> in the parish, and hence that pleasing confidence in your judgment
> and discretion which ought to be *mutually* entertained and
> *practised* between a minister and the people does not reign, nor
> do I, after the deepest and most anxious reflection, see a prospect
> of your establishing under existing circumstances at West Hartle-
> pool.

He continued in magisterial style, lecturing the young clergyman on his ignorance about the vicar's and people's wardens:

> I know not to what you refer when you say that I have called
> a meeting of *your* churchwarden and omitted the *people's* church-
> warden – I have never called, nor invited, a meeting of church-
> wardens since the Church was built; neither do I know – neither
> should I recognise if I did know – *your* churchwarden as contra-
> distinguished from the people's churchwarden. There is no such
> difference when once appointed, and I assuredly have yet to learn
> that any clergyman can claim a right in any particular church-
> warden who is merely to do the bidding of the clergyman – ...
> I hope I shall ever be ready to assist and support the clergyman
> at Christ Church, West Hartlepool, in all matters where I consider
> him to act with proper liberality in his views and conduct and
> when I see that he conducts matters both in and out of the Church
> with discretion and an avoidance of that suspicion and spirit of
> antagonism which I lament to witness in you as well to persons
> in this ecclesiastical district as to your neighbouring clergyman
> and his parish – though he, like yourself, is one of the ministers
> of the same religious establishment. He is not like minded in this
> respect towards you and your district; and I and others of my
> friends, as laymen, desire with our pecuniary means and otherwise
> as God enables us, to do the most extended good we can for the
> education *in all respects* of the children of the poorer population,
> which we have been the great means, humanly speaking, of
> congregating in, what must be generally called at present, "West
> Hartlepool". In this, for the purpose of such unusually large

National Schools, we include the *township of Stranton* in the first instance, almost in the very heart of which have we proposed to establish them; and I cannot see the fairness, and I regret the uncharitableness, of your conduct in originating a schism about a point or two of Ecclesiastical doctrine, or a difference of opinion between yourself and a neighbour on the interpretation of Scripture, which neither of you would obtrude in the education of poor young children, who are quite incompetent to understand such doctrinal points ... but, after the numerous alternative proposals which I made at the vestry on Saturday – all having for their object the most extended good for this *New Town*, and the whole of which met with your dissent unless *you* had the sole management and dictation in every respect as the minister, – I must candidly assure you I felt, and do feel, the strongest disinclination to support you in what appears to me, so selfish and contracted a course of reasoning and action. Neither do I perceive that if we erect National Schools a few yards from the present proposed site and just out of the line of your Ecclesiastical District, and desire equally to give to the children of that district the means of education as if the schools were in your district, you have any willingness to meet your laymen in that object. Hence I am bound to confess that you glaringly betray, in my opinion, a degree of obstinacy and perversion, which I am satisfied will be extremely obstructive to the well-being of this rising town.

He tried to end generously:

I know well you do not wish such a state of things; but I foresee that certain result.

I am sorry that, at last Saturday's meeting, trifling points of another kind were incidentally brought in. I admit they were irrelevant and should have been avoided.

I bear testimony to your zeal and your too hard working. I best know what I have expended out of my own pocket in hitherto promoting your wishes, and I am sensible, therefore, that I have not at least "gone against you".

Burges, disillusioned, replied promptly and curtly:

Nov. 21st. 1855
My Dear Sir.
I received your letter of the 20th instant. Upon good advice

I beg to say that I am unwilling to consent that the schools which I have collected money to build within the legally divided Ecclesiastical district of Christ Church, West Hartlepool, should be connected with any neighbouring parish. It is altogether contrary to precedent and ecclesiastical usage.

I therefore beg to say, if, upon memorial to the board and the West Hartlepool Harbour and Railway Company, generally and publicly, they revoke their grant of land, – the promise of which was made by you in the name of the company and attested by your signature to the Privy Council, – such shall be represented to the people of West Hartlepool, and the subject dropped for the present.

I am, Dear Sir,
Yours faithfully,
JOHN HART BURGES

This was not the kind of reply Jackson was accustomed to receive from one whom he had appointed and it must have made him realise that he was going to have trouble with this young man. He suggested that there should be a public meeting to hear both sides but, wisely, Burges ignored this. There was a rather pathetic attempt at intervention by Burges' curate, the Rev. E. L. Clark, who wrote to Jackson, "without mentioning the matter to anyone", describing the lack of education he had found amongst the children of "California", – "I found a large number of children without instruction of any kind and growing up in ignorance and not likely to become useful members of society" – and urging the great boon which he would confer if he would allow the schools to proceed. Jackson replied politely but firmly, suggesting that he did not understand the facts of the case.

Jackson demanded that the subscriptions collected by Burges should be handed over to what he called "the Schools Committee". Burges said there was no such legally-constituted committee but, without consulting Jackson, paid the money into a bank account in the joint names of himself, the Rev. John Lawson and the Rev. G. T. Fox. (Lawson and Fox, as soon as they heard of this, instructed the bank to remove their names from the account.) This greatly annoyed Jackson and he was further irritated when Burges wrote saying that he had received a letter from the Secretary of the Committee of the Council on Education "which I think will solve all our difficulties. I cannot tell you with what pleasure I have read it". The letter said no more than that there would be nothing to prevent children from another parish being admitted to the Christ Church Schools "so long as no children of the Parish mentioned in the trust are thereby excluded from the benefits of the School". In other words, so long as the Christ Church children had priority. This was not at all what Jackson was after, and Burges must surely have known it.

On the 11th of December, 1855, Jackson published a short statement giving his version of the dispute and it must have made Burges feel that discretion might be the better part of valour because, on the 14th of December he published a reply, in the form of a letter to Jackson, which said – "After our many conversations ... you surely cannot for a moment imagine that I ever *thought* of excluding the Stranton children, or those of any other Parish or creed whatsoever, from the benefits of education which, in co-operation with you, I have so much labored to procure for them". He repeated his view that it would be best for the schools to be Christ Church schools, but then he seemed to surrender, for he continued – "Having thus stated the views which have guided me throughout I beg to say I am willing to meet your wishes on the subject."

Jackson did not, as might have been expected, seize on this capitulation and translate it into practical effect. On the contrary he seemed to be in no hurry to bring the dispute to an end, for he replied to Burges repeating questions which he must have realised it would be difficult for Burges to answer. In particular the question which would be most likely to be unpalatable – "Do you mean that the Vicar of Stranton should be excluded from, or allowed to co-operate and be interested in any and what manner, in the proposed schools?"

Burges did not reply to that question but he confirmed his surrender in unambiguous terms:

December 15th, 1855

Dear Sir,

What I have all along objected to was the legally uniting two districts, lately legally separated, but *never* have I objected to the reception of the Stranton children. I have exerted myself for what I have believed to be the best, and have throughout taken the advice of others, for whose opinions I have the highest respect. I now beg to say I leave the management of the whole affair in your hands. I am sure you will allow, in all fairness, I can do no more.

Perhaps you will kindly let me know to whom you have sent your circulars, that I may send them a copy of my reply. Trusting we have now arrived at the end of this matter.

I am, Dear Sir,
Faithfully, yours,
JOHN HART BURGES

Surely that should have been the end of this matter – but it was not – very far from it! Perhaps Jackson had already learned something that made him scent a more resounding rout of this rector who had lost his good opinion.

The Awful Discovery

Whatever view one may take of the rights and wrongs of the dispute between Ralph Ward Jackson and the Incumbent he had appointed to Christ Church (and many may think that Jackson was fully justified in insisting that the schools should be available to all children of his town of West Hartlepool) surely few will have any sympathy with him in what he did after the Rev. Burges had given way to his wishes. Instead of accepting his surrender, he ignored it, and continued to publicise his differences with Burges. Then, in a letter to him dated the 31st of December, 1855, after referring to the correspondence which he proposed to publish, he included this strange and ominous paragraph:

The time has now obviously arrived, when it is proper that some mutual understanding should be come to for carrying out your retirement of which you have lately, on several occasions, given me intimation; and which, as the resident Trustee of Christ Church, I have no alternative but to accept.

Of course Burges had no wish to retire from his incumbency and there seems little doubt that Jackson was deliberately misinterpreting what Burges may have said about wanting to retire from the schools project. At all events, Burges put the matter beyond doubt by an immediate reply:

Dear Sir,
  To prevent any possibility of misconception on the subject I beg to inform you that I have no intention whatsoever of resigning the Incumbency of Christ Church, West Hartlepool.
Yours truly,
JOHN HART BURGES
Incumbent of Christ Church, West Hartlepool
December 31st 1855.

Jackson kept the pot boiling with correspondence about the schools, as if that were still the great issue between them, and Burges continued to demonstrate his awkwardness. In response to Jackson's demand that he should pay over the school fund, he transferred it into an account which he opened at Back-house's Bank in the names of all the members of the schools committee, plus those of the two churchwardens, plus those of himself and a newly-appointed curate (the Rev. W. S. Evans) – nine names in all!

Jackson published a second pamphlet, containing a continuation of his correspondence with Burges, and Burges published a letter dated the 9th of January, 1856, addressed to "his Parishioners, and the Public (explaining the real state of the School question in the Parish), occasioned by a Pamphlet lately published by Ralph Ward Jackson, Esq., entitled – "West Hartlepool Schools Correspondence". In it he gave the history of his involvement in the schools project and included this:

When all was now complete – the plans approved, and the

necessary funds obtained; I, as the Chairman appointed by the Committee of Council on Education, called together the Local Committee on the 17th November, for the purpose of advertising for tenders for the erection of the Buildings; when – the views of Mr. Jackson having changed – he, for the *first time*, demanded a total alteration of the Trust Deed, as approved by the Committee of Council, so as to insert "The Township of Stranton" in the place of "The District of West Hartlepool", thus changing altogether the destination of the money subscribed and of the grant obtained.

I now found myself, most unwillingly, obliged to differ in opinion from Mr. Jackson – for the following reasons:-

1stly. Because the funds having been collected for a special purpose, I did not conceive that either Mr. Jackson or myself were authorised to dispose of monies otherwise than strictly in accordance with the conditions upon which they had been given.

2ndly. Because the number of children in the District seemed fully to require Schools of the dimensions proposed. A sufficiently correct estimate of the number may be arrived at from the facts – that there are already over 500 children's names on my Sunday School Books; and we may fairly suppose, as many are taught in the Sunday Schools of other Denominations, of which, no doubt, a large majority would attend these Week-day Schools, and that there are about 7000 or 8000 inhabitants within the limits of the District.

3rdly. Because no child of the Township of Stranton, or any other Parish, could warrantably be refused admission to the Schools so long as there was a vacancy. – See clause III in the memorial. – See, also, opinion of the Secretary of the Committee of Council on Education, quoted in my circular of Decr. 14th.

The Stranton District would be likely, also, to suffer from this arrangement – inasmuch as a grant once obtained from the Privy Council, for that District, might prevent it from obtaining an additional grant, when additional Schools might be required. How much better and wiser then would it be for the inhabitants of Stranton to do as we have done, and obtain a grant for themselves sufficient for their wants.

These were my reasons for considering myself obliged to object to the change proposed by Mr. Jackson, especially at a time when a change of opinion could scarcely be considered justifiable.

Normanby Hall in 1980.

Greatham Hall.

But, – it may be asked, if, – holding these opinions, and believing it my duty, as Minister of this Parish, where the population is so rapidly increasing, to advocate and maintain the interests of the children of the Parishioners, not only for the present, but also for futurity. – Why did I afterwards concede to Mr. Jackson's subsequent demand?

The reasons which induced me to take this step, notwithstanding my mature and deliberate opinion as to the merits of the question, are as follow:–

1st. Mr. Jackson's decided refusal to *execute the conveyance* of the site for the Buildings, unless I complied with his altered views, without which, of course, the Schools could not be commenced.

2nd. The risk of losing the noble grant of £1983 to our District, which would be endangered by delay – as the conditions of that grant required the completion of the Schools within 18 months' from the date of its assignment.

3rd. The consideration that so large a number of children in the Town must grow up without education, if, through delay, the age for receiving instruction should pass by.

4th. My earnest desire for a peaceable arrangement of the matter on the best terms possible. In fact, I was forced to choose between two evils – either Schools according to Mr. Jackson's arrangement, or that the Parish should be left altogether without a School. Of these I thought it my duty to choose the least. But, allow me to remark that, although for these reasons I have taken this step, yet I would not wish to appear to the subscribers under the original arrangement, as desirous in any way to dictate to them the course they should now pursue in this matter. However, I may say that, for my part, I am now ready to assist in building Schools according to arrangements sanctioned by the Privy Council, in cases where Schools are built for the benefit of "more than one Parish", as set forth in "Minutes of the Committee of Council on Education, 1852–3," page 64; and, as I can make no further concession, I sincerely hope there may be no further delay in the erection of these much needed Schools.

He finished thus:

And – I appeal to you my friends – should a difference of opinion, upon such a question, embitter private feeling, or destroy the friendly relations which had hitherto subsisted between Mr.

Jackson and myself – the abruption of which I MOST DEEPLY REGRET.

Surely a matter of Public concernment should not occasion private animosity.

Meanwhile, secretly, Jackson was pursuing what had now become his determined aim – to get rid of Burges – and as a first step he was looking at the documents and the Acts of Parliament which had been used to assign a district to Christ Church and to appoint Burges as its Incumbent, and he had made a discovery which ought to have caused him the greatest concern for his own position in these matters but which, apparently, did not. Whether he had made it before the end of 1855 is uncertain, but there is strong evidence that he knew of it by the middle of January, 1856, for, on the 22nd of that month he wrote to his co-trustees, Lawson and Fox, suggesting that they should withdraw from the trust, as they would not wish to be mixed-up in the dispute with Burges and he had "now found that proceedings of a very decided character must shortly be taken". Both said that they had no wish to retire, so Jackson simply ignored them.

In the middle of the nineteenth century most people had very little security in their employment. They could be hired and fired without any restraint other than the protection of legally binding contracts. Judges were very secure but there were very few other classes of employees or office holders who could not be dismissed, except for offences of unlikely commission, and then only after lengthy Court investigation. Among these priviliged classes were the Incumbents of the Church of England. So Jackson's persistence in his quarrel with the Incumbent of Christ Church, after the latter's surrender in the school's dispute, was, on the face of it, puzzling and likely to lead only to the continuance and exacerbation of an unhappy relationship between the man who had created the church and the man who possessed the "parson's freehold" of it. Unless, by chance, there was a defect in the title to that freehold!

Jackson thought that he had discovered such a defect. If he was right, he was primarily responsible for it and an ordinary mortal in that position might have been tempted to leave the defect hidden or, more responsibly, to acknowledge it and to take the most urgent steps to rectify it. But Ralph Ward Jackson was no ordinary mortal.

The defect was simple but awful – it was, in fact, simply awful. It not only invalidated the Rev. Burges' title to his Incumbency but brought into question the validity of marriages solemnized in Christ Church. And many marriages had taken place during the twenty months since its consecration and they were continuing at an increasing rate from week to week. The defect was that the documents which Jackson had had prepared for the establishment of the church had been based upon, and submitted to the Bishop of Durham under, an Act of Parliament (1 & 2 Will. 4, c. 38, passed in 1831) which had been amended some three years before the documents were prepared by another Act (14 & 15 Vict. c. 97, passed in 1851). To make matters worse, the amending Act substituted the Church Building Commissioners for the bishops as the proper authority to assign districts and vest patronages for new churches. So it was obvious that everything that had been done to establish Christ Church, other than its consecration (which was a purely spiritual matter), was null, void and of no effect.

Jackson, almost certainly then in possession of this alarming knowledge, got his Town Improvement Commissioners to call a public meeting in the Atheneum on the evening of Tuesday, the 19th of February, 1856. The large hall was crowded with what the *Stockton and Hartlepool Mercury* called "a highly respectable audience". On the platform were seated Jackson with some of his fellow Commissioners, one of Jackson's brothers from London, R. W. Dixon, of Seaton, the Rev. Ridley, the Rev. Burges and his new curate, Mr. Evans, who had recently arrived in West Hartlepool from his native Ireland. Edward Turnbull was elected to the Chair. Burges tried to forestall the public relations exercise which was likely to take place by putting in a letter which he had received from the Council on Education, in reply to one written by him. It said that a Government Inspector would come to West Hartlepool in March to investigate the schools problem. This annoyed Jackson, and he delivered a long address in which he was painstakingly rude to both Burges and his new curate. He pretended that he did not know who Evans was, but soon contradicted this by referring with scorn and anger to the correspondence he had recently had with Evans about the banking of the schools fund, and also to the petition which Evans had organised and which was alleged to contain the signatures of 675 "principal tradesmen and others". It was addressed to Jackson and his Company and asked them not to delay the commencement of the building of the schools by withholding the site which had been promised for them.

Jackson did not disclose his sensational secret, but with the benefit of after-knowledge, it is possible to detect one or two clues that he possessed it. He did not, however, disguise his intent to get rid of Burges. He said:

> Now one reason why I cannot unite in any matter in which Mr. Burges has anything to do, is the fact of his absolutely refusing to recognise the ordinary arrangement of society in all matters of business, namely, a majority. [*i.e. a majority decision by the Schools Committee*].

He was referring to Burges' refusal to hand over the schools fund to him alone.

He spoke at length and to a sympathetic audience about his own liberal ideas with regard to the schools as compared with Burges' restricted views. He ignored the fact that Burges had surrendered in the dispute.

Burges, fearing that he would not be able to remain cool and collected in this Jackson-organised meeting, had written his speech. It emphasised that he had withdrawn from the schools argument and had left the field to Jackson. But by now he knew that Jackson's real object was to have him out of his living, and he gave his evidence:

Now, Gentlemen, give me your careful attention while I show you that the conclusion I have arrived at, with respect to the schools, is sound and reasonable. That conclusion, you will no doubt anticipate, is that the school question, from the very first, has been only a pretext to attempt my expulsion.

He described a conversation which, he said, had taken place between Jackson and the Vicar of Stranton on the evening of the day on which Burges' letter of surrender had been received:

Attend, Gentlemen, the fact I am about to state is of the utmost importance. Mr. Ridley welcomed him thus – "Well, Mr. Jackson, I see Mr. Burges has given in. I suppose everything is now settled." Gentlemen, what was Mr. Jackson's liberal reply? It was this – "Far from it, Mr. Ridley. He has given in, but now I won't work with him. I have broken fresh ground with him today." To use his own words, on the 9th, to two of the Church Trustees, "the cancer impeding the healthy action of the place must be cut out – Mr. Burges must be removed."

Burges, in his ignorance of what Jackson knew, added:

He knows that no power in the land can move me from my incumbency.

Jackson was allowed a reply, but when Burges tried to speak again he was told that the meeting had gone on too long, and indeed it had, for it lasted nearly five hours and broke up just before midnight. As it reached its closing stages, one of Jackson's colleagues, William Ramsey, moved that Burges should retire from Christ Church so that the building of the schools might proceed, but this proposition, said the *Mercury*, "was received by a perfect storm of hisses and groans". That having failed, a further motion, that a committee, consisting of Jackson, Ralph Walker, C. Wigham, Edward Turnbull, C. Emerson, John Pile, Mr. Lisle, Mr. Lowden, Mr. Richardson, Mr. Casebourne, Dr. Kirk, Dr. Oldham, W. Ramsey, Mr. Armstrong, Mr. Duncan, Mr. Wise and Mr. Baker, with power to co-opt, should be set-up "in order to facilitate the establishment of the schools", was passed unanimously.

The *Mercury* report concluded:

> Mr. Burges, at this moment, rose and advancing to the table, said he had agreed to everything Mr. Jackson had asked, and wás now willing to shake hands, and forget all about it. (*Loud applause*). No reply was made on the part of Mr. Jackson.

Before this meeting had been arranged, it would seem, Jackson, or his London Agents, had prepared a Case for Counsel's Opinion to get confirmation of the view which he had formed about the illegality of the constitution of Christ Church, and this was submitted to three eminent Counsel. They soon gave the confirmation which he wanted.

Then, acting in the manner of a dictator, he moved swiftly and secretly to secure the reins of power to his own hands. He could trust the Vicar of Stranton to be his confederate and, with him, hurried to Blagdon, in Northumberland, where lived Ridley's brother and patron, Sir Matthew White Ridley. They easily persuaded him that, in the circumstances, it would be best for the patronage of Christ Church to be vested in Jackson alone, and he signed a document to this effect, which Jackson had had approved by Counsel. It may be asked why Sir Matthew had the power to do this. The answer is that, if the documents for Christ Church were void, then that building, being consecrated, was a chapel within the Parish of Stranton and, as such, came within the patronage of Stranton.

The transfer of the patronage to Jackson needed the endorsement of the Church Building Commissioners and of the Bishop of Durham. The first was a formality, the second might be more difficult to obtain.

On the 19th of March, 1856, Jackson's London Agents wrote to the diocesan deputy registrar, Joseph Davison, blandly telling him of the legal mess that had occurred, not accepting a tittle of responsibility for it, but implying that it was the fault of Davison himself and of the Bishop, whom it was his duty to advise, and dropping in the frightening hint that not one hour must be lost in getting the Bishop to approve the transfer of the patronage to Jackson so that everything could be put in order as quickly as possible, because marriages were still being solemnized in the church and this could not be done "without, to say the least, giving rise to doubts to which we will not further advert". They gave no indication that Jackson's co-trustees had not been consulted. The Bishop, in a letter to Jackson some months later, said that Davison was ill at the time and had simply passed on the document, along with many other things for the Bishop's signature and that he, being nearly blind and in poor health, relied without question upon the propriety of signing the things submitted to him without knowing what they were about.

There can be no doubt that Davison knew what was the effect of the document, but he may not have been told that the co-trustees had not been consulted. Jackson had been so anxious to obtain the Bishop's endorsement that not only had he himself written to Davison, but he had made the railway journey to Durham on Saturday, the 22nd of March, and had seen him and, no doubt, had reinforced the veiled imputation of his London Agents that Davison was responsible for the mess and, if he did not promptly get the Bishop's signature, unintended immorality might continue in West Hartlepool and children be procreated whose legitimacy would, to say the least, be doubtful.

Jackson was relieved to be told by Davison that the transfer would be endorsed that very day.

Up to this point he had not said one word to the man who would be most affected by the mistake that had been made and who could not, by any stretch of the imagination, be considered in any way to blame for it – the Rev. John Hart Burges. Nor had any word been said to the co-trustees who, with Jackson, had been responsible for the selection and appointment of the clergyman. But now, at last, he thought Burges might safely by told.

How the Bad News was Broken

Immediately on his return from Durham on Saturday, the

22nd of March, 1856, Jackson sent a message to Burges asking him to come to his office, as he had something important to tell him, not connected with the schools. Burges did not respond. So, on the evening of that day he took the Vicar of Stranton to Burges' house in Albert Terrace and there he found Burges in company with his curate, the Rev. Evans. Jackson and Ridley spent three hours trying to drill into poor Burges' head that he was not really the Incumbent of Christ Church; that he was not licensed to perform the offices and sacraments of the Church in that building; and that he was, by solemnizing weddings, occasioning the unmentionable. Burges could not and would not accept a word of it. He knew, only too well, that Jackson was now his enemy and anxious to get him out of West Hartlepool. He said he would continue his Ministry unless and until the Bishop withdrew his licence.

The meeting ended with Jackson and the Vicar of Stranton drawing-up a notice which they said they would post on the doors of the church. It read:

NOTICE

Marriages churchings and baptisms cannot take place in Christ Church, West Hartlepool, until further notice. For these offices of the Church parties must, in the meantime, repair to the parish church of Stranton, which will be open for marriages every day from 8 o'clock a.m. to 12, except on Sundays, when it will be open from 8 a.m. to 10 only (all banns of marriage must be published in the parish church of Stranton). For baptisms and churchings the parish church will be open every Wednesday and Friday at 11 o'clock a.m. On Sundays, at 2 o'clock p.m. except on the first Sunday of each month, when the parties must be at the church 10 minutes before 3 o'clock p.m.

Punctuality is particularly requested.

RALPH WARD JACKSON
Patron of Christ Church, West Hartlepool.

H. R. RIDLEY
Vicar of the Parish of Stranton

West Hartlepool, March 22nd, 1856.

As this notice had been drafted under Burges's nose he prepared to counter it with this:

NOTICE

Marriages, baptisms, churchings, etc. will be solemnized as usual in Christ Church, West Hartlepool, as long as the Bishop of Durham's licence to the incumbent of Christ Church remains unrevoked.

JOHN HART BURGES
Incumbent of Christ Church,
West Hartlepool
22nd March 1856.

And so, "before Divine Service", as Jackson put it, on Sunday, the 23rd of March, 1856 these two notices were fastened on the doors of Christ Church by their respective authors, or their supporters. It must have been a rather distracted congregation that attended the Service of Mattins that Sunday morning.

The notices remained on the doors for a few days, but, on the Sunday following, an agitated Vicar of Stranton wrote to Jackson – "Our notice has been taken down; I understand another marriage was celebrated this morning. You cannot allow this to go on, I mean the marriages."

It was all very well for the Rev. Ridley to say that, but what could Jackson do if this recalcitrant young clergyman refused to obey his orders? To try to get a legally binding order against him in an Ecclesiastical Court, even if possible, would have been a long-drawn-out proceeding. However Burges had said he would obey the Bishop, so the obvious thing to do was to get the Bishop to withdraw his licence.

But first, having heard that Burges had consulted a Stockton solicitor, J. R. Wilson, Jackson had no hesitation in approaching that solicitor for an interview – "Pray do not suppose that I wish to intervene in the slightest degree but I shall be most happy to afford you every information I can towards your understanding of the matter." He suggested that Wilson should come to his room in West Hartlepool and, on Wilson's excusing himself from that, went over to Stockton and saw him there. Within three days Wilson had written to Jackson, "I gave my opinion very firmly to Mr. Burges and advised him to resign at once. He had gone to see the Bishop and I conjured him not to get into a mess there or he would do himself an everlasting injury." After another few days he wrote again "I begin to suspect he is not satisfied with my advice and has gone to some one else." No wonder!

So Jackson had to embark on the task of trying to persuade the Bishop to withdraw Burges' licence and, to his annoyance, found that that was going to be much more difficult than he had expected. In fact it soon became apparent that, of the clergy involved in the matter, only the Vicar of Stranton was sympathetic to Jackson's cause. All the others – the Vicar of Seaton Carew, the Rev. Fox, Archdeacon Bland and the Bishop himself – seemed to take the perverse view that the responsibility for the mistake which had been made was primarily Jackson's and that he had acted improperly by not consulting his co-trustees. Furthermore they suggested, and it was indeed obvious, that there were simple ways of rectifying the mistake without the withdrawal of the Rev. Burges' licence or his dismissal from the living of Christ Church. Jackson was astonished to get a letter from the Vicar of Seaton Carew which upbraided him in no uncertain terms for his want of courtesy to his co-trustees, his breach of faith towards the public, his gross injustice towards Mr. Burges and his arbitrary conduct towards the people of West Hartlepool. Such denunciations from a resident of West Hartlepool would have been treasonable but the Rev. Lawson was outside the kingdom, so he was told – "It appears to me you are unnecessarily interfering with a locality with which you have no official or other connection, Seaton being your own proper and sufficient scene and sphere of usefulness ... It is clear that you have withdrawn yourself from all possibility of connection with the church or me." He had been banished!

In his implacable opposition to Burges and his determination to have him out of West Hartlepool, Jackson spared no effort. During the three months which followed the posting of the notices on the doors of Christ Church he wrote nearly sixty letters to Burges, Davison, Lawson, Fox, Archdeacon Bland and the Bishop. Many were very long, some more than four foolscap pages. He made railway journeys to Durham, Bishop Auckland and London. When he heard that Archdeacon Bland was to discuss the matter with the Bishop he contrived a visit to a solicitor in Bishop Auckland and sat in his office, hoping to be called to the meeting. When no invitation had arrived by mid-morning he sent another note, by hand, but the Bishop and the Archdeacon were cautious and would not see him.

All this activity achieved nothing, except to frighten the Bishop sufficiently for him to advise Burges, at the end of April, 1856, to discontinue marrying until the legal doubts were cleared-up.

As the correspondence and the comings-and-goings continued the tone became more frigid and, on Jackson's part, more threatening. From the middle of May he repeatedly warned that he would have no alternative but to close the church. The Bishop cautioned him against any such action. The Deputy Registrar suggested a simple remedy that would have allowed marriages to continue in the church. This would merely have required an application from the Patron and the Vicar of Stranton for the Bishop to license Christ Church as a chapel within the Parish of Stranton for the purpose of celebrating marriages. The Bishop was ready to grant the licence and Davison had gone to the trouble of preparing the application, which he sent to the Rev. Ridley. This solution to what Jackson had so often urged as the crying need for the Bishop to withdraw Burges' licence exposed his real purpose and, as soon as he had heard of Davison's suggestion, he wrote direct to the Bishop rejecting any such solution "which I am convinced is uncalled for under existing circumstances and would only tend further to complicate the whole matter and increase the difficulties as to a complete remedy." Six days later the Rev. Ridley dodged the issue by writing to Davison suggesting that his brother was the one who should be consulted.

Jackson thus made no bones about it – he would not have Burges on any consideration, and any remedy which allowed him to stay at Christ Church was, for him, unacceptable. And, as he had the patronage in his own hands, nobody could do anything about that. But neither could Jackson rid himself of this rejected priest – unless, perhaps he resorted to physical means. And that was not out of the question for Ralph Ward Jackson, as he would demonstrate on several occasions during his stormy career in the North East.

As early as May, 1856, he had threatened the Bishop that he would publish the correspondence and had asked for the Bishop's, Archdeacon Bland's and the Deputy Registrar's agreement. All of them refused but that did not deter him, and he published all the correspondence in a pamphlet dated the 27th of June, 1856.

In his last letter to the Deputy Registrar, dated the 26th of June and written from London, he said:

> The subject is fairly exhausted by correspondence; and I now bring it to a close, with the expression of my deepest regret that I should, in any manner, be mixed up in a scene which I am sure is calculated to bring upon our Established Church a most degrading exhibition – a result which I conscientiously feel I have done everything in my power to avert.

The Battle for Christ Church

The extraordinary events that took place in Christ Church and its vicinity in July and August, 1856, have not been related in detail in any of the histories of West Hartlepool but they were narrated in newspapers circulating in the locality. They were also described in letters to the Press written by Jackson and by "Fiat Justitia". As might be expected these accounts are not identical.

It was some diversion to the literate public of those days (who had no television, wireless, cinemas, motorcars, bingo halls, night clubs or football teams) that the Press was quite uninhibited in its partisanship of individuals and causes, and largely oblivious of the dangers of libel or the kinds of journalistic ethics which now suppress the hearty abuse and withering scorn which enlivened the columns of such papers as the *Stockton and Hartlepool Mercury and Middlesbrough News*, the *Durham Chronicle*, the *Durham Advertiser* and the *Sunderland Times*.

The *Stockton and Hartlepool Mercury and Middlesbrough News* was a blatant supporter of Ralph Ward Jackson. The Rev. John Hart Burges' brother (who also was a clergyman), alleged that it was in his pocket. Benjamin Coleman was another who said that the paper was Jackson's own, or in his service. The *Mercury* contemptuously denied these charges and said that the small amount of advertising revenue that came its way from Jackson's Company was of little moment to it. The *Mercury* also said that the *Durham Chronicle* only started to sell in West Hartlepool after the Christ Church affair had become a scandal and implied that it was the tool of the ecclesiastical influences in Durham.

What follows is an account of the events as described in the *Mercury* and the other sources. Where there are significant differences the source will be indicated and the *Mercury's* own words will be used to narrate the happenings on Wednesday, the 30th of July.

During nearly the whole of July there had been a deceptive lull, but the storm broke during the early hours of Tuesday, the 29th of July, when Jackson's workmen descended on the church and fastened locks on all its doors.

The *Mercury* of the 2nd August, 1856 tells its story:

RIOTOUS PROCEEDINGS AT CHRIST CHURCH, WEST HARTLEPOOL

We have this week to record the transaction of outrages in connection with Christ Church, West Hartlepool, which cannot but awaken the most painful reflections in all sensible minds. The dispute betwixt Ralph Ward Jackson, Esq., patron and founder of this church, and the Rev. John Hart Burges, its Incumbent, has certainly attained a climax, and threatens not to close without mischief to the sacred edifice itself.

It is well known that for several weeks past Mr. Jackson has been in communication with dignitaries of the church, to arrange, if he possibly could, the removal of Mr. Burges without resorting to measures more rigorous and extreme. In this attempt, however, he failed; and came to the determination of excluding the Rev. Gentleman by fastening up the doors of the church; Mr. Burges meanwhile industriously assuring his friends in every quarter that no such steps durst be taken. As a matter of course, most of the inhabitants were on the "tip-toe of expectation" as to how the matter would end. On Tuesday last, however, to the general surprise of Mr. Burges' friends, the doors were fastened up, and the following announcement, conspicuously painted on a board, appeared in the church-yard:–

Notice, – In consequence of the invalidity of the document as to Christ Church, West Hartlepool, no marriages, christenings or baptisms, can legally take place in it, nor is any clergyman, whatever, authorised to perform them. No ecclesiastical district has been assigned to Christ Church, West Hartlepool, and no minister has been duly appointed or licensed to perform services in it, and inasmuch as the Rev. John Hart Burges assumes to officiate contrary to law and without having obtained the requisite consents of all parties, it is necessary and proper that this building should be closed (and which is done with great reluctance), until all proper and legal documents and authority be obtained. It will be opened as soon as these matters are satisfactorily arranged. Any persons wishing books or other articles can have them on application.

Henry Richard Ridley.
Vicar of Stranton
Ralph Ward Jackson,
Patron of Christ Church.
West Hartlepool, July 29th, 1856.

Tuesday passed without any public manifestation of feeling or display of opposition to the course adopted by Mr. Jackson. But

Mr. Burges and his friends were not quiescent. Everywhere it was made known – and the intelligence spread with characteristic haste – that the following (Wednesday) morning the doors would be broken open, and an entrance to the Church effected by force. Mr. Burges had appealed to the Churchwardens to insist on the church being opened, or to sanction a forcible entrance. Dr. Atkinson refused to move in the matter either way, and declined becoming a party to any steps that might be taken; whilst the decision of his colleague, Mr. Harrison, remains a secret. It is certain, however, that Mr. Burges procured a party to break off the lock of the door at the Western entrance; Mr. Harrison, we understand, being present at the time, and – according to general report – lending his sanction to the deed. We have interrogated him subsequently, ourselves, on the subject, but have failed to ascertain whether such is the case or not. And now comes "the tug of war." The church was entered in triumph by the Rev. gentleman, amid the congratulatory exclamations of a "devoted" band of followers – men, women, and children – the women displaying the most unbounded enthusiasm. The locks were now wrenched from the doors at the south and eastern porches, one of which was barricaded by the insertion of a strong rib of wood between the door and the opposite wall. The doors were then thrown open, the crowd inside shouting to them that were out "come in, come in", very much as Bunyan's Pilgrim heard them from the top of the palace "Beautiful" – the only difference being that the invitation was not given in exactly a similar spirit. Intelligence of these proceedings having reached the ears of Mr. Jackson, in company with his son, Mr. Wm. Jackson, and one or two other gentlemen, he proceeded to the spot to expostulate with Mr. Burges, and challenge his authority for breaking open the doors of the church. The *rencontre* of the two gentlemen was attended by an incident which has been the subject of considerable exaggeration. Whilst Mr. Jackson was questioning Mr. Harrison as to whether he had ordered the forcing of the doors or not, Mr. Burges interposed to tender some explanation or offer an argument, when Mr. Jackson pushed him quietly aside with his hand, requesting him not to interfere. Mr. Burges, however, persisted in obtruding his person and remarks, and the gentle push with the hand was repeated twice, accompanied by a request that he would stand back or Mr. Jackson would compel him to do so, which elicited an angry retort from the Rev. gentleman. Mr. Jackson, finding he could gain no satisfactory information as to who had authorised the opening of the church, and having listened patiently to a plaintive harangue from Mr. Burges, retired expressing his resolution to take away the doors altogether, and wall up the entrances.

The intelligence of this spread wild-fire like; rumour, with its arithmetical taste for compound-addition, adding that Mr. Jackson had struck the Revd. gentleman three violent blows on the stomach! This story in our hearing went through a score of different versions, and ended like that of the three black crows; for one of our own agents, on whose recital we can place confidence, assures us that Mr. Jackson laid his hand on Mr. Burges with nothing more than the moderate touch a man would use in putting his friend aside. Presently, however, a body of men arrived, – of what *class* the sequel discovers – and the doors being lifted from their hinges were carried away; Mr. Burges being engaged at the time in churching a woman. His sympathisers were loud in their expressions of disapprobation, and women, mothers of families with children in their arms, and maidens of the Juliet time of life, wandered up and down the church declaring they wouldn't go home, even to cook the family dinner, alternatively, thanking heaven there was cold meat in the house, and venting anathemas on Mr. Jackson and blessings on the priest. But one and all resolved that they would not leave the church, even though they should be walled up within it. Things now began to look extremely awkward; and as the throng inside increased in numbers, cushions and books were removed from the seats by their owners or their servants, and the interior of the sacred building presented a graphic sight. Mr. Burges was, of course, "the observed of all observers", and the eyes of his "faithful followers" watched his movements with evident impatience and curiousity. The Rev. Mr. Charge, of Coxhoe, too – who remained in the church a great portion of the day in company with his brother-minister – was an object of frequent remark amongst the crowd. Suddenly, about half-past one, they retired together into the vestry, and then anxiety grew to fever height. "What is it?" was the general cry, and presently somebody spread the news that the Telegraph Company had refused to transmit a message on the subject to the Archdeacon. And then woe betide the Company if the women could have had their way, and they were only in earnest when we overheard them. Let our readers picture a body of directors dangling from a row of telegraphic posts, and then they will have an idea of these matronly intentions. We took it for granted, however, that this rumour was purely a fiction, though it gained ground throughout the day, and was very generally believed.

But the *fracas* had not yet reached its culminating point. About two o'clock a body of masons arrived, equipped with their tools, and preceded by two or three cartloads of bricks, which were deposited opposite the several porches. Their arrival was the signal for shouts, hisses and tumult; but they proceeded with as much despatch as they could to brick up the entrances, relays of bricks continuing to arrive. By this time the church was crowded with a regular (i.e. irregular) mob, some of them strong athletic fellows of undoubted pluck, and eager for a "bit-of-fun" – the sport, however, being evidently confined to the active members of the mob, many respectable onlookers expressing only disgust at the misapplied frivolity and irreverent riot. Mr. Burges was away at the cemetery, officiating at a funeral, where he expected to be opposed. The workmen laboured away at the walls, some twenty inches thick, and soon had them say half a yard from the ground or more. Then arose the shouts inside of "Down with the walls, lads," "Down with 'em," and the mob cheered and clapped their hands till the sweat ran down their faces. The strongest fellows who were there now took a ladder which had been conveyed into the church, and, using it as a battering-ram, sallied down the aisle, urged on by the throng behind, and, with a force that was irresistible, swept down the newly-built wall at the western end of the church, resounding with cheers. The women then turned up the sleeves of their dresses, and, with broiling faces, pitched out the bricks, relieving each other by turns. The men renewed their charge with the battering-ram at the other entrance, whither the women again followed them, and renewed the game of "pitch and toss." The scene at this moment baffles description. The ladder, – or battering-ram, as the reader likes – was brought in triumph and raised perpendicularly in the centre of the aisle in proximity to the altar rails, when the ringleader who had headed the "storming of the walls" ran up to the top of it, his comrades steadying it without any other support but their hands. He then waved his cap as a signal, when three tremendous cheers were

given, succeeded by the cry of "Chair him, chair him," and the
hero only escaped a very critical ride on the summit of the ladder
by making a rapid descent. Then ensued a scene such as is, happily,
rarely enacted under the roof of a religious temple. The mob were
rushing to and fro over the tops of the sittings; fictitious marriages
were celebrated at the altar; mock sermons addressed from the
pulpit, the mimic priests indulging in the luxury of a cutty pipe;
whilst mimic baptisms took place at the font. The men shouted
that they must have some beer, and the tumult that existed was
never outdone by tap-room, theatre, or fair. At intervals the bells
were tolled in requiem style by amateur ringers, and a flag of
distress was hoisted on the top of the tower. The labourers, finding
it useless to renew their task, desisted from building up the walls
again; and the iron gate leading into the churchyard was thereupon
locked by one of Mr. Jackson's officials, and carefully guarded.
Those who were inside were permitted to come out, but everything
was done to prevent any of the impatient outsiders from entering.
Many who were refused admission, however, scrambled over the
rails in spite of the prohibition issued; but on the arrival of Mr.
Burges from the cemetery, the gates were opened for him, and
the mob refused to allow them to be closed again, though a strong
effort was made for that purpose. The indignation of the Rev.
gentleman's adherents was now increased by the assurance from
his own lips that Mr. Jackson, Mr. Ridley, and their friends were
proceeding to the cemetery to oppose his conducting the funeral
service there; but that he had completed the ceremony before their
approach. Of course we give this as we heard it detailed by Mr.
Burges himself. Up to midnight the same scene of excitement was
kept up with the usual incidents peculiar to mobs in general; and
we have reason to know that Mr. Jackson would have interfered
with the police to put an end to proceedings so disgraceful and
so inimical to the sacred purposes of the church, had he not been
withheld by fears lest the building should itself be mutilated.
Throughout the whole affair on Wednesday nothing was more
striking than the excited and sometimes violent demeanour of the
women – with few exceptions, all of the lower orders – who
evidently would not have hesitated to pull down the church with
their own hands if the signal had been given.

But if the day's proceedings, which we have detailed without
the slightest exaggeration, were outrageous and disgraceful, they

were utterly eclipsed by those of the night. The mob with which the church was filled consisted of the lowest and most ruffianly men – drunken sailors, Irishmen and "navvies". They wandered up and down the church, in and out of the pulpit and pews and within the altar railing – shouting, whistling and smoking. A mock marriage was celebrated by a drunken sailor, he declaring it to be "the only legal marriage that had been celebrated in that church", a remark which was greeted by the mob with three hearty cheers. Two "navvies" then ensconced themselves in the pulpit; and after enjoying their pipes to the great diversion of the crowd below, one of them laid hold of a prayer-book and harangued the mob, amidst tumultuous shouts of laughter and bravos. Meanwhile a brother navvy, self-delegated to the office of priest, was baptising an infant at the font. Hassocks were pitched about in every direction; the building rang with cheers and laughter, and the drunken oaths and fiendish threats that mingled in the uproar gave a crowning effect to the Pandemonium-like scene. The awful and disgusting threats uttered against Mr. Jackson by many of the women offer the truest index to the character of the matronly enthusiasts in the cause of the rev. gentleman. They were, in fact – at least those which we heard ourselves – too revolting for repetition. The mob manifested no inclination to retire; and about nine o'clock Mr. Burges, who had been in the church while these scandalous and disgraceful proceedings were in progress, made his appearance in the churchyard, thanked the mob for their presence and support, and expressed a wish that they would retire for the night. Three cheers were then given, and he left the scene followed by the more sober part of the crowd – the rioters retreating into the church again, evidently bent on further "fun". Such a sight as the church that night presented was never before witnessed. A drunken rabble from the races swelled the ranks of the mob; and a strong desire was expressed to tear up the seats and commence the destruction of the sacred edifice. Hundreds were smoking short pipes and cigars, all sorts of farcical tricks were played, and from the communion table and pulpit Christianity was ridiculed; and the most solemn rites of the church burlesqued. Such were the men and such the doings that elicited the gratitude and called forth the thanks of a "Christian" minister.

In its next weekly issue the *Mercury* stated that "after the

mêlée on Wednesday, no further effort was made to build up
the entrances. But detachments of the rabble continued to
linger in and about the church up to Sunday, on which day
divine service was celebrated in it by Mr. Burges. Both morning
and evening the attendance was crowded, the majority of the
congregation being strangers from Seaton Carew, old Hartlepool and the immediate neighbourhood." What they did not
report, until considerably later, and then only incidentally to
an account of a prosecution in the magistrates' court, was that
on the day after the attempted bricking up of the entrances,
a Mr. Newbiggin, a shipbroker in the town, had marched upon
the church at the head of a body of pilots and, in an attempt
to retake it from Burges' supporters, had assaulted the sexton.
Newbiggin was prosecuted for assault and, although the
Mercury described the incident as "a lark", the magistrates
evidently thought it serious enough to fine him £4 with 10s.
6d. costs – a substantial penalty in those days.

On Sunday (the 3rd August) there was a rumour that
Jackson intended to make another attempt to take possession
of the church by force and the Rev. Lawson, on hearing of
it, sent an urgent message to Rowland Burdon of Castle Eden
(a County Magistrate) urging that he should arrange for the
attendance of a sufficient body of police to prevent bloodshed.
Rowland Burdon, with the Rev. J. A. Park, Vicar of Elwick,
immediately went to Greatham Hall and saw Jackson. He
satisfied them that it was only a rumour. Nevertheless there
arrived by rail at West Hartlepool some large blocks of lime-
stone and some of Jackson's workmen hinted that they had
been intended for the purpose of blocking up the entrances.

On the same Sunday evening Rowland Burdon summoned
a meeting, attended by the Rev. Park, some County Magistrates (J. P. Denton, R. W. Dixon, and S. Robinson), the town
clerk of Hartlepool (Thomas Belk) and representatives of the
police, to discuss the situation.

The next morning (Monday the 4th of August) Jackson went
before the district magistrates at Castle Eden and requested
the presence of a sufficient staff of police to take charge of

Christ Church. His application was not granted, but on the evening of that Monday a second consultation took place at which Major White (Chief Constable) assisted and at which it was decided to keep a large force of police in the town to protect the church. On Tuesday night, therefore, Mr. Burges' watchers were withdrawn and the policemen quietly brought into the neighbourhood of the church for its protection. The next day (Wednesday the 6th of August) Jackson, the Vicar of Stranton, the Rev. Park, the Rev. Burges and the Rev. Fox had a meeting with Archdeacon Thorp and he was asked to arbitrate in the dispute. On the same day three representatives of the West Hartlepool Improvement Commissioners (Allison, Ramsay and Baxter), waited on the Archdeacon and urged the necessity of the suspension of religious services in the church. They got no satisfaction, but next day the Archdeacon gave his decision to Jackson:

> I am clearly of opinion that the doors of Christ Church should be restored by you, and the services continued without interruption by the licensed curate, Mr. Burges, till the questions of right, now in dispute, are arranged by mutual consent, or determined by due course of law.

Jackson took more than a month to comply with that decision and, even then, he did so only imperfectly.

Psychological Warfare

Having been defeated in the physical confrontation between his forces and those of the Rev. Burges, Jackson next resorted to psychological warfare. If he could not close the church he would try to drive the congregation from it. He wrote a long letter, dated the 13th of August 1856, to the *Stockton and Hartlepool Mercury* and to the *Durham Advertiser* and also had it printed and circulated. It opens in regal style:

TO THE INHABITANTS OF WEST HARTLEPOOL
I deem it appropriate at the present time thus to address you.

It gave Jackson's version of the Christ Church affair up to

the time of the locking of the doors and then went on to outdo the *Mercury's* description of what was alleged to have happened afterwards:

> What followed? A Christian Minister – instead of appealing to any of the Ecclesiastical or other authorities surrounding him – but guided by his own intemperate feelings and the countenance of two other Ministers of Religion, though in no manner connected with West Hartlepool, and not supported by a single respectable inhabitant of the Town – rushed, with excited impetuosity, violently to break open every door of the Church, admitted a large mob and rabble, who had assembled by previous notice of his intended proceedings, and afterwards, by his presence, countenanced and encouraged the most obscene and foul abominations which were ever perpetrated in a Building destined to be "a house of prayer" and a place for the Worship of Almighty God.
>
> That scenes and pollutions of the vilest character – known only in the brothel and lowest pot-house – occurred uninterrupted within the walls of that Building – within its Pulpit and Reading-desk – within its Baptismal Font and the precincts of the Altar; that Religion was scandalized – the Ceremonies of the Church mocked, and fornication and other beastliness practised within the very Altar rails and other parts of the Building – are FACTS, attested by an overwhelming amount of evidence; whilst it is equally well proved that, at a late hour of one of the evenings when those atrocities were occurring, the mob – the perpetrators of them – were thanked by the reverend Mr. Burges for their presence and support; and, at another time, congratulated at his having, at all events, by such assistance kept possession of the Church!
>
> I can only assert that I never was near the Building when these abominations took place, and most assuredly I did not know of their extent until after they had occurred.
>
> In now addressing you I feel bound, as a man and a Christian, to express my deepest indignation at these occurrences. The very thought of them is revolting in the highest degree; and it appears to me that it is impossible and most indelicate for any chaste, modest, or Christian mind ever to enter within the walls of that degraded and disgraced Building, until some of the polluted portions of the interior be removed, and until, by some Public

countenance of a Dignitary of the Church, *he* shall proclaim by *his* presence and *his* preaching, that Peace and Harmony have been restored to it – that it is, in all respects, in a fit and proper state for Religious Worship, and that all documents necessary and proper to give it a legal constitution, with undoubted licences for all services in it, have been completed, so as to establish it in all future time as "a house of prayer" and a Church of England.

What father or mother, what son or daughter, what brother or sister, – nay, what man or woman of any chaste mind and right feeling can, under the present state of things, and before some such outward and visible sign of purification be adopted, make up their minds to enter that Building, – to listen to the welcoming toll of its bells, – to sit on its benches, – approach or look on its polluted Altar and its furniture, – hear the word of God read and professed to be preached from its desecrated Reading-desk and Pulpit, – and join with one heart and mind in a solemn worship, – and to reconcile it to themselves and their consciences that they can do all these things with composure, comfort, devotion and prayer? It is, I say, impossible and I pity the inconsistency, the hypocrisy, the indelicacy, and the conduct of that person, who may now countenance, or participate in, any religious services in that Building in its present degraded condition; – for a Church it is not in any sense of the word."

And then Jackson disclosed his proposal to buy-out Burges:

Much as I feel there is just ground for objection to Mr. Burges' conduct, and that it has also been such towards myself and family, as to preclude me from ever appointing him to the future ministry of Christ Church – when purged and purified as far as human means can devise; – and though the invalidity of the License, which the Bishop has by error granted to him, seems an acknowledged fact, yet I have deemed it a Christian part to convey to Mr. Burges that, notwithstanding all that he has said and done and all that has passed, I am willing to consider his present pecuniary means and future prospects, and that, if he would retire from the sad scene which West Hartlepool presents, without giving further trouble or pain, I will agree to allow him £150 a year clear, until by my own, or his, or his friends' instrumentality, he obtains a living, or Curacy elsewhere, which shall yield him not less than £150 a year.

I have stated that I have made such offer, without prejudice to any person and solely in the "Interest of Peace", as I feel sure every one must now be sensible that his retirement from West Hartlepool is absolutely necessary for the peace, the welfare, and good of the Town.

I am glad to be enabled to say that I have received a Letter from Archdeacon Thorp, stating that "my proposal in Mr. Burges' favour is very handsome and considerate, and must be so regarded whatever be the issue."

I can scarcely now believe that any respectable and thinking person in West Hartlepool can be of a different opinion, – not only as to the course he ought himself to take, and urge upon Mr. Burges to adopt, but as to the offer I have myself made to him: for it effectually answers and disposes of the assertions, I know he has made everywhere, of my injuring him pecuniarily.

Having, however, satisfied my own feelings and conscience by spontaneously making such an offer to Mr. Burges for the sake of peace, I will wait for a reasonable time for its acceptance, or rejection. If the former, I shall be ready at once to carry it out in every honourable manner. If the latter, it can only perpetuate the discord, the scandal, and insult now occasioned by Mr. Burges and his few supporters; but it must not, in such case, be expected that I and my family at least can any longer place ourselves in a position to witness and receive the continuance of such conduct: other measures of a decided and painful character must then ensue.

I remain,

Your faithful friend,

RA: WARD JACKSON.

During August, 1856 the *Durham Chronicle* published two letters signed "Fiat Justitia", part of the contents of which have been mentioned on previous pages. As might be expected, they give a different account of the circumstances which led to Burges' appointment to the incumbency of Christ Church and of the schools dispute, and they refute the allegations about the scenes which Jackson had described in his published letter. The following are extracts:

(*Referring to the legal flaw*) – All men are liable to error; and a good man, and a man of honour, who falls into it, will rejoice when he finds it is in his own power to rectify it; but, if the error were in his favour, would be hurt and shocked at the bare idea of any one supposing he could take advantage of his own wrong. No doubt a man so clever as Mr. Jackson, the moment he was aware of the flaw, was also aware that the remedy was in his own hands: two of his co-trustees were his father-in-law and his brother-in-law; and the remaining two, the Rev. G. T. Fox and the Rev. John Lawson, even had their feeling in favour of Mr. Burges changed, which it had not, would have blushed to take advantage of a clerical error, so that there could have been no difficulty in complying with the provisions of 14 and 15 Vic. c. 97. It is deeply to be regretted that the better feelings of Mr. Jackson did not impel him at once to do so, and thus correct his own error. Had another been the patron, and he only acting as attorney, he could not have been ignorant that if, through his blunder, he gave his client a bad title, he was liable to him in damages. He had here the opportunity of adding to his popularity – he has most unwisely forfeited it. Instead of consulting his co-trustees he went, in company with his friend the Rev. Mr. Ridley, over to Blagdon, and got himself appointed the sole patron of Christ Church; and with considerable address and adroitness, behind the backs of those most interested, procured from the unsuspecting proper authorities the confirmation of his appointment.

(*referring to the attempt to brick-up the entrances.*):

... I will not extend this letter by recapitulating the disgraceful scenes enacted at Christ Church, in Mr. Jackson's presence, and by his command. Those who are interested in the question, and do not desire to see a minister of the gospel trampled under foot, and a mere puppet in the hands of a lay patron, (though that patron has also the patronage and physical force at his disposal which attach to him as chairman of a railway and dock company), will probably take care to prevent a recurrence of the outrage, and may even make the cause of the persecuted minister their own, and bring to judgment the violator of the Sanctuary. I am no enemy of Mr. Jackson's. When he was guarded from the attack on Christ Church to the railway station, I fancy I can picture the agony with which he would say, *"Populus me sibilet!"** for he is one who desires *"digito monstrari"*† and he is of sterner mould than his friend and coadjutor Mr. Ridley, who, after putting police officers in his house, to protect it from imaginary danger, fled to the more elegant and quiet retreat of Harrogate. I have given you facts: I believe they cannot be controverted. Mr. Jackson has not, as yet, denied any of them; he has contented himself with evading all discussion on *his own* acts, and has confined his attention to dishonest interpretations or ingenious criticisms on the writings and conduct of others. He has expatiated on the "grievous injury" and "the wrong and scandal" going on at West Hartlepool in connection with the church, but chooses to overlook that *he* is the sole author of and responsible for both.

He forgets, also, that while passion will not allow him to search his own heart, and examine the motives that have led to his late conduct, others, both in West Hartlepool and out of it, are doing so; and that having, by letters in the newspapers, and his selected published correspondence, put himself upon trial before the public, the manly, independent, and generous portion of it have long since given their verdict against him; and that even those in West Hartlepool, who are connected with him in his public capacities, and have their prosperity bound up with his, and who think, and not unfairly, that he is the creative genius of the place, cannot help sometimes asking one another, whether it is essential for the prosperity of their town that their benefactor should be the Bishop of it as well as the King!

....

Again, Mr. Jackson has misrepresented Mr. Burges' conduct by saying that "guided by his own intemperate feelings, he rushed with excited impetuosity violently to break open every door of the church." Now, I don't hesitate to say that this is a most gross perversion of the truth. Mr. Jackson had, by barricading or otherwise fastening up the doors of the church (an act which neither an Incumbent nor Patron has a right to do), broken the law; and before he charged another with doing so, it would have been more candid had he acknowledged his own fault; but it is utterly untrue that Mr. Burges "rushed with impetuosity to break open the

*The people hiss me.   † To be pointed out.

doors." *He* did not break open a single door; but finding that the doors had during the night been fastened, he discharged his duty in a proper and strictly legal manner, by calling on the churchwardens to have them opened – for, as many of your readers will know, the churchwardens are the officers of the parish in ecclesiastical affairs, as the constables are in civil, and are, moreover, the guardians or keepers of the church, and the legal representatives of the parish body – as see laid down in "Prideaux's Duties of Churchwardens", page 1, and "Blackstone's Commentaries", vol i, p. 394. Mr. Jackson has, however, prudently, though not very honestly, suppressed all reference to his own illegal and discreditable conduct subsequent to the opening of the church doors. It was, however, quite needless to tell the inhabitants of West Hartlepool the tale, so well known to them already, of his violent and insulting language and conduct towards Mr. Burges in the church, and how, against all law and decency, he caused the church doors to be torn off, and the door-ways built up with bricks. He, an educated man, having from his official situation force at his beck, appealed to physical force and broke the laws of his country: can he now seriously complain that his example was followed, and that a mob, collected to watch his proceedings – hearing that their beautiful church was threatened, and their faithful minister assaulted – should, without waiting to reflect, on the impulse of the moment, rush to the rescue? That they committed no violence, is attested by the fact that not a single pane of glass was broken, nor the slightest injury done either to the fabric or the ornamental parts of the church – a fact that stands in bold relief and graceful contrast to the acts of unlawful and ruthless violence committed by Mr. Jackson.

I must also charge upon Mr. Jackson gross exaggeration and wilful perversion of the scenes which afterwards took place. As a "man and a Christian", for so he speaks of himself, he describes, in very coarse and indecent language, shameful and wicked "abominations" as taking place inside the church when he was not near it; and he ventures to say that these "are FACTS attested by an overwhelming amount of evidence". I will not sully this paper nor shock the reader by repeating here what he has written. If they are *facts* as he alleges, they can be proved. I challenge him to the proof. For the sake of the peace of the place, which he has broken; for the sake of its purity and decency, which he has outraged; nay, on behalf of the Minister, whom he has cruelly injured, I call upon him to substantiate *his* "*facts*". Let him ask the Chancellor of the Diocese, and the Chairman of the County Sessions, with three or four other County Magistrates unconnected with West Hartlepool and its trade, to sit as a Committee of Inquiry to receive evidence on his shameful and disgusting charges, including in its sacrilegious abominations "*fornication*", for so he expressly asserts, and I promise him he shall be met face to face; that the groundlessness and falsity of his charges shall be exposed and laid bare, and the originator or inventor of the scandalous tale detected and disgraced. The report and sentence of an honourable Committee, so constituted, will carry weight. Will Mr. Jackson seek and abide its decision? But has it never struck Mr. Jackson, that if those scenes which he so complacently describes *did* take place, that they lie at his own door, and are the not unnatural consequence of his own acts, and therefore that he, of all men in the world, should have been the last to have exaggerated the offences committed in consequence of them. If a man wantonly or wickedly takes away his neighbour's gate, or breaks down his hedge, so that cattle stray in and destroy his corn, is not the former legally, as well as morally, liable in damages? Where is the difference between the two cases. Mr. Jackson has torn down and taken away every door of the church; those doors which alone could keep out a mob. He has gone further. Contrary to the remonstrance and express injunction of the Archdeacon, he refuses to bring them back. What is there but the awe-felt respect towards the "House of God" which prevents this church from nightly being the resting-place of the wanderer and wretched, or the scene of those orgies which Mr. Jackson's imagination has conjured up?

In another part of his letter, Mr. Jackson states that "Mr. Burges thanked the mob". This statement is untrue. Mr. Burges denies it *in toto*, and denied it explicitly in Mr. Jackson's presence, when therewith charged by that gentleman.

And lastly, Mr. Jackson makes a great flourish of trumpets about a most liberal offer of £150 a year to Mr. Burges to retire. This offer would have come with a better grace if Mr. Jackson had first settled with Mr. Burges for the monies already due to him; besides which, it is couched in such slippery terms as would enable Mr. Jackson to escape from all responsibility, and leave Mr. Burges in the lurch. For instance, suppose Mr. Jackson offered

Mr. Burges a *curacy* of the specified amount, either in a most unhealthy district, or under a most unsatisfactory incumbent, or that, if accepted, Mr. Jackson's friend, who provided the curacy for Mr. Burges, turned him off at the end of six months – in any one of these cases, Mr. Jackson might say his liability was at an end. Yet this is what he calls a very liberal offer. He expects Mr. Burges to resign a living which ought to be worth £200 a year at the least, to which he was most honourably presented, where he has faithfully discharged his duties and is greatly beloved by the people, to enable him to gratify his own selfish wishes; and he makes Mr. Burges an offer which practically is worth nothing. But why should Mr. Burges resign at all? Is he to surrender his status as Incumbent of West Hartlepool, to rend the ties by which he is united to the people, and to become a *Curate*, in order to gratify Mr. Jackson's ambition, and enable him to exercise, as lay patron, a power which he has acquired by a most dishonourable course of proceedings, and which would probably be taken from him, were he to submit the questions in issue to the jurisdiction of a Court of Equity?

I have now, Sir, reviewed and answered the principal topics in a letter which Mr. Jackson's real friends must regret he ever wrote and circulated. In doing so, I have only taken up my pen to vindicate the cause of truth, and put fairly before the public the conduct of a Lay Patron towards a Clergyman whom he had himself selected. By the inhabitants of West Hartlepool, where oppression seeks to stifle the voice of truth, and where threats and promises are used to estrange the people from their Minister, I shall be pardoned for the caution –

> "The bold untruths, which you are forced to hear,
> Receive discreetly with a patient ear."

But to Mr. Jackson I will also give a word of caution and advice. Let him, before it is too late, pause in his career and retrace his steps. Let him redeem his honour, and thus regain his popularity. Let him make reparation where reparation is due, and all will be forgiven and forgotten. In doing so, he will give ease to his troubled spirit, quiet the apprehensions of an accusing conscience, and restore to his breast peace and happiness. Should he neglect this advice, I warn him that his hold on the respect of the people of West Hartlepool, already weakened, will be broken; and that, as the sad tale circulates at a distance, and amongst the public, there will be found many who will hazard speculations as to the confidence to be reposed in his honour as the Chairman of a public company, should they believe that in this unhappy instance he has forfeited and made shipwreck of it.

I remain, Sir, your obedient servant,

FIAT JUSTITIA

With hindsight, it is, perhaps, tempting to attach more significance to the warning in the last paragraph of this letter than is justified.

On the 23rd of August, 1856, the *Mercury* had a leader which referred to the "very handsome offer" made to Burges to secure his retirement and reported that a meeting had been held in the Atheneum at which Mr. Kirk, surgeon, presided and Messrs. Harrison and Atkinson (churchwardens), Crosby, Richardson, Davidson, Emerson, "etc., etc." were present. As a result a petition, urging Burges to accept the offer, had been deposited at the Atheneum and "yesterday had nearly 300 names attached – comprising most of the leading professional men, merchants and tradesmen of the town". It also divulged that, three days before the Atheneum meeting, the West Hartlepool Improvement Commissioners had discussed the proposed petition and all those present had signed it. This was hardly surprising, Jackson being their Chairman. The next issue of the *Mercury* reported that the petition, containing 330 signatures, had been presented to Burges on the 28th of August but he had already prepared a written reply which said that, having been placed in the Incumbency of Christ Church by Mr. Jackson and his co-trustees, and "having no reason to suppose that my ministrations have been distasteful or useless to my flock, I have no intention of betraying the trust reposed in me and I shall not resign the living so long as I have the approbation of my Diocesan and am able efficiently to discharge my pastoral duties".

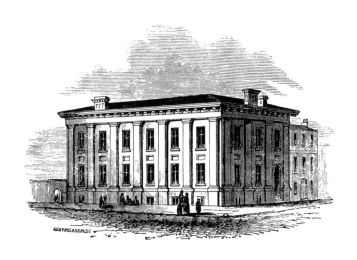

ATHENÆUM.

The Atheneum as it was planned and built in 1852.

The Atheneum as it was in 1978.

Christ Church from the West in 1978, with the statue of William Gray in the foreground. (Originally the churchyard was larger, rectangular in shape and surrounded by heavy iron railings.)

The Battle in the Cemetery

Town planning is not an art or science of new invention. It was practised by individual land developers many years ago and among the town planners of the Industrial Revolution was Ralph Ward Jackson, operating, of course, through his Company. In his mind's eye the town to serve his harbour and railway must have a cemetery to replace the already overtaxed churchyard of All Saints, Stranton. And he, being an ingenious man, had realised that he could kill two birds with one stone. A prime necessity of his new harbour and dock would be a dumping ground for the soil, sand and rubble which must be excavated to create them, and such a mound, if properly arranged, would be ideal for a burial ground. So the Hartlepool West Harbour and Dock Company acquired the land which is now the North, or Hart Road, Cemetery, and the workmen's cottages which became known as "California", were deliberately placed at the western extremity of this land, so that the remainder could be used for dumping. By 1854 the mound extended over an area of eleven acres and the West Hartlepool Improvement Commissioners had been established as the local authority for the new town. One of their first acts was to buy the eleven acres from Jackson's Company – tipping having been completed, and to build a lodge at the eastern end (this was not at the present Hart Road entrance, but on the crest of the incline which leads from that entrance).

Part of the cemetery was consecrated for Anglican burials and the Bishop of Durham licensed the Rev. Burges, as the incumbent of Christ Church (in whose district the cemetery lay), to bury the dead in the consecrated ground. The cemetery was first used at the end of April, 1856, when the Christ Church dispute was moving towards its climax. It was under the control of the Improvement Commissioners, and Jackson was their Chairman.

The battle between him and Burges was not confined to Christ Church and its precincts – it soon moved also to the cemetery and took the form of attempts to prevent Burges from conducting funerals, on the ground that he was not the lawfully constituted incumbent of the church.

How determined Jackson became in his efforts in this direction and how scandalous became the results, may be gleaned from the following report which was published in the *Mercury* on Saturday, the 6th of September, 1856.

FRACAS AT THE WEST HARTLEPOOL CEMETERY

In our report in another column of a special meeting of the West Hartlepool Improvement Commissioners, held on Wednesday last, will be found a description of a painful and discreditable funeral scene at the cemetery, arising from the Christ Church dispute. The account there given is verified by several of the Commissioners who were spectators of what took place; and corresponds exactly with as much of it as we witnessed ourselves. The exact position of affairs relative to this dispute is too well known to need recapitulation here; we may, however, briefly remark that the Town Commissioners, convinced that there is no legal district of Christ Church, and, consequently, no legal Incumbent, as Mr. Burges professes himself to be, have more than once forwarded a resolution to him protesting against his interfering with the funeral services at the cemetery, inasmuch as Mr. Ridley, the Vicar of Stranton, (there being no district) was alone entitled by Act of Parliament to bury the dead belonging to his parish. The Commissioners, it will be borne in mind, simply wished Mr. Burges to refrain from interfering till the legality or illegality of his title was established by a proper tribunal. Being informed that a funeral would take place on Sunday last, several of the Commissioners, amongst whom was Mr. Ralph Ward Jackson, their Chairman, accompanied by his son, Mr. Wm. Jackson, proceeded to the cemetery for the purpose of protesting against any infraction of their order on the part of Mr. Burges. On arriving they found Mr. Burges there and ready surpliced nearly half an hour before the time appointed. Mr. Jackson encountered him as he was on the point of emerging from the room of the lodge; and entering it, closed the door, and, placing his back against it, handed Mr. B. a written remonstrance from the Commissioners, which he had some difficulty in persuading him to read. He then requested him to take off the Commissioners' surplice, or he should not leave the room; and although there were other people in the apartment with him, the rev. gentleman ran passionately from one window to another shouting out "murder, murder", (though nobody was touching him, or offering to do so) and knocked violently on the panes, beseeching the people outside to rescue him. All this is matter of fact, which admits of no contradiction. Mr. Ridley, on his arrival about four o'clock, entered the room, put on the other surplice, and had commenced reading the service, when the father of the child that was to be buried, and who was unmistakeably drunk, snatched up the coffin, and declared he would take it home again. Just before this he had assured the spectators in stammering tones, that he had a pistol in his pocket to prevent Mr. Ridley performing the service. The exhibition he then made reflects the deepest disgrace upon him. He reeled about with the coffin under his arm in a most excited manner, once slipping on his knee with it, and refused to listen to the entreaties of his wife and the other mourners who tried to pacify him. Mr. Jackson very courteously asked him if he had agreed with Mr. Burges to bury the child, and on learning that he had, informed Mr. Ridley of it, who, in the most gentlemanly manner possible, relinquished the office into the hands of Mr. Burges, and at once retired, accompanied by Mr. Jackson and his son. The only unseemly features of the occurrence were the ludicrous screams of Mr. Burges, at which even "thick-lipped, musing melancholy" must smile; the unmatronly ravings of one or two "women friends" of the rev. gentleman, who on this, as on other recent occasions, would have figured far more honourably, if less conspicuously, at home; and the deplorable spectacle which the intoxicated father of the dead child presented. With these exceptions, no symptoms of riot or disturbance were visible.

How the War was Won

All the battles, so far, seemed to have ended with victory for Burges. But Jackson had not done. He had two trump cards, and was now playing them.

He had withheld from Burges the greater part of what should

have been his income. He had not invested the endowment fund but retained it in his own control – a matter about which the Rev. Fox wrote to him in strong terms. He had, improperly, instructed the churchwardens that they must, before paying to Burges the pew rents, deduct from them the choir expenses, the organist's salary and other expenses. And he had deprived Burges of his rent-free house in Albert Terrace, but would not allow him to occupy the parsonage, which had been completed at the beginning of 1856, but had since stood empty and locked, with instructions from Jackson to his employees that if Burges "presumed to enter it" they were to use "such reasonable force as might be necessary" to eject him from the building. This notwithstanding that the building of the parsonage had been a task assigned by Jackson to Burges and he had obtained promises of grants from the "Maltby Fund" and Queen Anne's bounty. But when the time came to enter into a building contract Jackson had deleted Burges' name from it and substituted his own and he had also retained the title to the site.

These were dreadful measures which it would have been difficult enough for Burges to withstand but perhaps what made him feel that he could not continue the struggle was the retirement of his most powerful ally, Bishop Edward Maltby. He had become nearly blind and had, in December, 1855, executed a power of attorney to enable the Bishop of Manchester, Archdeacon Bland and a Rev. Mr. Douglas to carry out some of his functions. His death was not far away. How much the Christ Church affair contributed to his decline can only be guessed, but it would not be surprising if the awful mess to which he had unintentionally contributed, preyed on his mind. He retired in October, 1856, and was succeeded by Dr. C. T. Longley, who was enthroned in the third week in November.

Burges must have felt that his life-line had parted, for, however sympathetic Dr. Longley might be towards him, he could not have the same feeling of responsibility for his situation as had Bishop Maltby. And the scandal of Christ

Church must be brought to an end somehow if the Church of England were not to be brought into disrepute.

Burges' apprehension was justified. The *Mercury* had reported on the 13th of September that:

> The unhappy proceedings in connection with this place of worship (Christ Church) are assuming a better appearance ... The Venerable and esteemed Diocesan, doubtless determined to bequeath the Bishopric to his successor unsullied by so miserable an imbroglio ... has, we understand, intimated to Mr. Burges his desire that he should retire ... This, we hope, is the beginning of the end ...

Depressing as this must have been to Burges, it had the opposite effect on Jackson, who felt sufficiently reassured by it to comply, in part, with what Archdeacon Thorp had told him to do some six weeks earlier. The *Mercury* contained a copy of a letter, dated the 9th of September, from him to Burges which, after referring to the Archdeacon's recommendation, said:

> I have therefore, towards the preservation of the building, and without prejudice, fixed the doors to it this morning, with new locks to replace those broken by you. I have also, today, written to the Archdeacon informing him ... I have also stated to him that I retain the keys in consequence of what has passed with reference to yourself and your own conduct – of the illegality of the license and the other documents.

In spite of the pressure on him, Burges did not yet yield. His friends had rallied to his aid. The *Durham Chronicle* reported:

> A meeting of the *real friends* of the Rev. J. H. Burges was held on the 17th of September at half past seven when resolutions were passed expressive of sympathy and confidence and likewise for the purpose of raising a fund in consequence of the proper funds of the living being withheld from him and he being deprived of his present dwellinghouse, which he has occupied, rent free, ever since he came to West Hartlepool.

And, in January 1857, the same paper reported that a meeting had been held in the Mayor's room in Durham on Wednesday, the 14th of January, for the purpose of authorising the treasurer of the fund to pay over a portion of the subscriptions which had been collected:

> The proceedings were quite of a formal character, and did not occupy more than a few minutes. The Rev. G. T. Fox moved, and Mr. John Shields seconded a proposition that J. H. Forster Esq., be authorised to pay over to Mr. Burges the sum of £200 and the remainder when the accounts are made up. This was at once assented to, and the business concluded.

But the end was near. On Saturday, the 28th of March, 1857, the *Mercury* had this:

> The last chapter in the Christ Church Drama – at least we should hope so, for the sake of peace, and even for the reputation of those concerned – has just developed itself. On Sunday evening last [*22nd March*] the Rev. John Hart Burges preached his farewell sermon. A crowded congregation, including a large number of strangers, were present. The discourse was of an eminently practical character. On Wednesday evening, a public meeting of the rev. gentleman's friends was held in the class-room of the Atheneum – Mr. John Richardson in the chair – at which the following address was presented by the chairman, and arrangements were made by the female portion of the audience for getting up a ladies' testimonial to Mr. Burgess [*sic*]:
>
> An Address to the Rev. John Hart Burgess on his leaving West Hartlepool; Presented at a Public Meeting, held in the Atheneum on the 25th of March 1857, –
>
> Reverend Sir – In the name of a very large number of the Congregation of Christ Church, West Hartlepool, and also of the vast mass of the inhabitants of this town of all religious denominations, we beg, on the eve of your departure from among us, to express to you the deep feelings of respect we entertain towards you. Without entering at all, at this late period, into the merits of the recent controversy, we beg to assure you that it is with feelings of the utmost regret that we learn that the relationship which has so long subsisted between you and us is now to be severed. We have been no inattentive observers of the unceasing

solicitude you have at all times evinced for the spiritual welfare of your people, whilst your many acts of unostentatious charity have also shown your desire to promote their temporal good. At the chamber of the sick, and at the bed of the dying, have you ever been ready to bring the blessed comforts of religious consolation – night and day have your willing services been at the disposal of the sick, the needy and the afflicted. These many acts of Christian pastorship, as well as your bold, unflinching exposition of the truths of Christianity, have engendered in the hearts of your parishioners a very fervent feeling of esteem and affection. Whilst we sympathise with you upon your sudden removal from among us, we yet congratulate you that the decision of your spiritual superior is based solely on legal reasons, and that not the slightest charge is substantiated against your character. All imputations upon you recoil only on those from whom they arose. Be assured, sir, that wherever you go, the sympathy of your parishioners accompany you, and their best prayer and wishes will be for your unceasing welfare. On this, the last occasion when we may ever meet, accept then, in conclusion, our best thanks for your faithful ministration, our deep sympathy on your removal from us, and our earnest hopes for your future happiness.

That could not be allowed to go unanswered. A month later, (the 25th of April) the *Mercury* contained this:

The following documents, which sufficiently explain themselves, have been forwarded to us for publication:

To Ralph Ward Jackson, Esquire

Sir, we, the undersigned, Members of the Church of England, Ratepayers and Inhabitants of West Hartlepool of all religious denominations, desire to convey to you our warm congratulations on the termination of the long protracted and unhappy dispute with the Rev. Mr. Burges.

While we deeply sympathise with yourself for all the pain and anxiety you have undergone during the past sixteen months, we cannot withhold the warm expression of our admiration of the characterisitic energy and resolution with which, alone and single-handed (strong only in the respect and esteem of your fellow townsmen), you have fought against an unprincipled combination of factious rivals and ecclesiastical partisans, until at last, after unexampled difficulties, you have succeeded in removing a standing source of bitterness and strife from this new and rising town.

Although we are not unmindful of the large pecuniary outlay which you must necessarily have incurred, nor of the disinterested liberality which has dictated the surrendering of the Parsonage [*sic*] of Christ Church to the See of Durham, we, nevertheless, feel persuaded that the consciousness of the great benefits which your untiring exertions in the late dispute have conferred upon this growing community (for whose existence here today you are mainly responsible) will prove an ample source of compensation for all the sacrifice you have been called upon to make, and will enable you to treat with merited indifference, the calumny and misrepresentations to which you have been so undeservedly exposed.

Upon the children of the poor of all denominations residing in West Hartlepool your uncompromising hostility to Mr. Burges' narrow-minded and sectarian views has conferred an inestimable boon and blessing. We are sensible that to your exertions alone is the town of West Hartlepool indebted for the liberal and comprehensive scheme of National Education (so rich in promise for the future) which we trust will soon be inaugurated amongst us; and, when the petty excitements and animosities of the hour shall have passed away, and reason and judgment resume their wonted sway, we feel assured that, in the contemplation of a happy and reunited congregation and of a peaceable and prosperous town, you will see ample justification for the part, which you have thought it your duty to take, in the painful drama (now so happily for all of us) brought to a close.

With the most earnest wishes for your continued health, happiness, and prosperity, we beg to subscribe ourselves,

Your sincere Friends and Fellow-townsmen.
April 21st 1857.

The above Address, which received the signatures of upwards of 600 of the principal heads of families, representing in the aggregate considerably more than three-fourths of the rateable value of property in the town, was presented to Mr. Jackson at West Hartlepool on Tuesday last by a deputation consisting of Messrs. Oldham, Hutton and Emerson, and has elicited the following reply:

Greatham Hall,
21st April, 1857.

Gentlemen –

I have the honour to acknowledge, with unfeigned pleasure and gratitude, the memorial you have today so kindly presented to me.

It not only eloquently and forcibly expresses your feelings upon the termination of the long and painful dispute with the Rev. Mr. Burges, but it also conveys, in generous and impressive terms, your kindly sympathy with myself and family on that happy event.

It is far from my wish at this moment to revive the painful feelings and associations which, during the late controversy, have been unhappily too rife, but I cannot allow the present opportunity to pass without remarking that I have, throughout, been fully sensible of the influences – other than religious or ecclesiastical – which have been at work in support of Mr. Burges, and which became very conspicuous in the subscription that was set on foot to enable him to prolong the contest in West Hartlepool.

It was certainly to be regretted that any such "factious rivalry" as that to which you have alluded should have been introduced into a question with the merits of which parties at a distance were necessarily but imperfectly acquainted, and, in some instances, entirely ignorant of them – and it is a still greater cause for regret that persons so remotely interested and unaffected should have been instrumental in prolonging, – or at all events embittering a strife the consequence of which – however prejudicial to the interest of the people of West Hartlepool – *they* could not possibly be made to feel it.

With reference to the allusion so kindly made in your address, "to the part which I have felt it my duty to take in the late dispute", I can only say that having been by most painful experience, impressed with the conviction that the retirement of Mr. Burges from West Hartlepool, was essential to the peace and progress of the town, and being strengthened in that conviction by the earnest appeal for his removal which, in conjunction with the late Bishop of Durham, I received from nearly the whole body of the pew-renters of Christ Church, it would have been an act of moral cowardice on my part, and unpardonable injustice to them, if I had attempted to shirk or evade the responsibility, which the error of the ecclesiastical authorities had thrown upon me and I need scarcely assure you that the additional testimony of your hearty approval and congratulations, conveyed by your present address, so very generously and influentially signed, is most grateful and acceptable to my feelings and is, indeed, "an ample compensation for all the misrepresentations and calumny to which I have been exposed".

Upon one point which has been suggested to me by your address – namely the reference to my having voluntarily transferred the patronage of Christ Church, in perpetuity, to the See of Durham, I deem it appropriate to say a few words, even at the risk of repeating what I have felt it to be my duty to say before.

I took upon myself, with members of my own family, the entire trouble, control and responsibility of building Christ Church, and I have altogether contributed out of my own pocket between £5,000 and £6,000, or more than three-fourths of the entire outlay.

At that time I had not acquired any experience in the establishment of new churches, and, previous to the consecration of Christ Church, I was impressed with the idea that my best mode of disposing of the patronage was to vest it in trustees.

I did not undertake the building of the Church, nor ever intended to take the patronage of it, for any private interest of my own or of my family – my only object being simply to do that which was most likely to conduce to the usefulness and prosperity of the Church and to the general interest and advantage of the town.

My views respecting a trusteeship for a church – circumstanced as Christ Church is – had from great experience and observation of such matters, undergone a most decided change; and I felt, what I still feel, that in a body of trustees so constituted, there is a great danger if dissentions and private animosities, which, when occurring, must necessarily cause – as has been lamentably exhibited in the case of Christ Church – very serious embarrassment and injury in administering so delicate and responsible a trust.

As therefore, *no trusteeship was in fact ever legally established for Christ Church* and as none of the four gentlemen I had asked to join me in such a trust had ever acted or interfered either in the building of the church or in any arrangement whatever connected with it, I came to the conclusion that it would be best for the interests of all parties to annex the patronage to the See of Durham in perpetuity; and I have accordingly made proposals to the present

Bishop of Durham for that purpose in order that the exercise of the power of nominating Incumbents to Christ Church in all time, should be vested in some responsible authority in a public situation.

Having given you these explanations it only remains for me in conclusion to express the hope that, as the dispute which has so long disturbed the peace and tranquillity of the town has at last been terminated by the intervention of the highest Ecclesiastical authority of the Diocese, all parties will again unite harmoniously in the promotion of those various works and institutions of usefulness which the growing necessities of the town demand, and that by the exercise of mutual forbearance and Christian charity, one towards another, we may, as a community be once more permitted to enjoy those inestimable advantages which peace, good-will, and a common purpose and interest never fail to secure.

Believe me, with every sentiment of gratitude and respect, ever your true and faithful friend.

RA: WARD JACKSON

Thus ended the dreadful contest between a man who, with some justification, thought he owned a harbour, docks and town which he had created, and a young clergyman whom he had appointed to serve his town and whose offence was no more than a short-lived opposition to one of his schemes. Those who feel inclined to judge should first read the whole of the story in this book, when they will discover that, as with most men, vices are tempered with virtues.

Charles Dickens was writing some of his most popular novels at about the time these events took place and he knew that his readers expected that all the best stories should have a happy ending. His efforts to contrive this were sometimes more than credulity could accommodate. Fortunately it is not necessary to invent in order to provide a happy ending to the Christ Church saga.

The Rev. John Hart Burges left West Hartlepool to become vicar of Bishop Ryder's Church, Birmingham. In 1867 he was awarded the degree of Doctor of Divinity and, after serving seventeen years at Birmingham he became Rector of Devizes. He stayed there for twenty-five years and died in office on the 23rd of December, 1899, aged 73. He had married late in life and left a young family, two boys and a girl, and a widow who survived him by 35 years. His younger son, Eric was killed in action at Ypres on his 23rd birthday.

As soon as Burges had left West Hartlepool his place was filled by the Rev. J. G. Rowe, but before the latter could have the Incumbency of Christ Church, Jackson had to put its affairs in order. This he did with his accustomed energy.

First, to end the agonising doubts which by then must have filled the minds of more than a few couples who had believed that they had been married in Christ Church between April, 1854 and April, 1856 (i.e. between the consecration of the church and the date when the Bishop told Burges to stop marrying) he promoted a private Bill which received the Royal Assent on the 10th of August, 1857 (20 & 21 Vict. cap. 29). It is entitled, *An Act to render valid certain Marriages in Christ Church, West Hartlepool, in the Parish of Stranton in the County of Durham*, and provides, in sec. I. that "All Marriages heretofore solemnized in the said Church, and the Publication of Banns in such Church previous to any such Marriage, shall be and be deemed to have been as good, valid, and effectual in the Law, to all Intents and Purposes whatsoever, as if such Marriages had been solemnized and such Publications of Banns had taken place in the Parish Church of Stranton". And, in Sec. II – "No Minister who has solemnized any of the said Marriages shall be liable to any Ecclesiastical Censures, or to any other Proceedings or Penalties whatsoever, by reason of his having so as aforesaid solemnized the same respectively."

The proposed transfer of the patronage of Christ Church to the Bishops of Durham, which Jackson had mentioned in his published letter of the 21st of April, 1857, was completed in July, 1858.

Finally, on the 11th of January, 1859, a District was assigned to Christ Church by Order in Council. By then Ridley had left All Saints, Stranton, and his place had been taken by the celebrated Parson Rudd.

Thus was good order and respectability established and Christ Church entered on its century of being the central Anglican Church of West Hartlepool, flourishing until after the First World War, in whose font the infant Compton MacKenzie was Christened in 1883 and in which, in its heyday, crowded congregations assembled to hear the preaching of such divines as Canon Cosgrave and Canon Macdonald.

As for the schools, no sooner had Burges gone than Jackson laid the foundation stone (28th April, 1857). The site was adjacent to Church Square and immediately opposite the church. It is now occupied by the College of Art. The schools committee, including such important people as Jackson's son, Thomas Casebourne, William Hutton, John Richardson, Ralph Walker, Cuthbert Emerson, William Ramsey, Christopher Salmon, John Pile and, of course, the Vicar of Stranton, were present. Jackson, as a final act of self-justification, placed in a bottle which was deposited in the foundation stone, a piece of parchment which said:

> The first stone of this building in which this record shall be enclosed was laid on Tuesday the 28th of April, 1857, being the twentieth year of the reign of our Sovereign Lady Victoria by the Chairman and Committee whose names are attached hereto. Created to establish and carry out schools which shall be accessible to the Children of the Poor to the number of Seven hundred and fifty from all parts of the Township of Stranton and Brearton within the Parish of Stranton without religious distinction and without compulsion as to the teaching of any religious formulary not approved by the Parents or Guardians of any child. The Chairman and Committee to be chosen from time to time from among the Inhabitants of all religious denominations whose position in the Community shall entitle them to election.

And now the new stone vicarage in Church Square, which Jackson had refused to allow Burges to occupy, could be made available to the Rev. Rowe. It stood where Barclay's Bank now stands. It had a garden surrounding it but was a rather dismal house, last occupied by Canon and Mrs. Poole.

How the Arch-Enemy was Made

While Ralph Ward Jackson was pursuing, with such energy and determination, his feud against the young John Hart Burges he was by no means idle in more important, and less vindictive, endeavours. As the fight was developing he was commencing the construction of his third dock, the Swainson, and building the huge warehouse that would adjoin it. He was making strenuous efforts to extend his railway into the Cleveland ironstone field. He was enmeshing himself in a web of future difficulties by various irregularities in the management and financing of his company. And he was Chairman of the recently-formed West Hartlepool Improvement Commissioners – the first substantial local authority for his new town – who had a large backlog of problems to deal with. Surely his mind must have been occupied by all these matters, and troubled by some of them. How, in the midst of all this he could have been bothered, or have found time, to carry his battle against Burges to victory, is reason, not only for astonishment, but also for reflection that here perhaps lay one of the clues to the cause of his ultimate downfall. He seems to have been subject to obsessions and to an inability to see the wood for the trees – to realise what was worth-while and possible and what was trivial and impracticable.

But, at this distance in time, it is a rather poignant thought that what directly caused his downfall was the result of acts of brotherly protection, well-meaning and unselfish.

It is ironical that, in the very years when Ralph was building his first harbour and dock, and thus laying the foundation-stone for his dream of a Liverpool on the east coast, his younger brother, Edwin, was, unknown to him, and in that same City of Liverpool, getting himself into the scrape that would ultimately spell disaster for Ralph. It happened thus:

Edwin had for some years prior to 1845 been living in Liverpool and carrying on a sketchy sort of business as a "broker". That is to say he would buy for resale "produce", or anything else that he thought might make him a profit. In 1843 he married a lady of fortune and retired from business. During 1845 and 1846 he gambled on the Stock Market and, for that purpose, employed as his stockbroker the firm of Coleman and Todd – a not very distinguished firm which had only commenced as a partnership in 1844, and which dissolved in 1848. The partners were Thomas Todd and Benjamin Coleman and, on the dissolution, Coleman took over all the assets. During those years, 1845 and 1846, there was a great deal of speculation and Edwin Ward Jackson bought and sold shares on a credit account with the firm. When the account was closed it showed a debt from Jackson to the firm of £1,210. 12s. 6d. which they claimed from him. He repudiated it and counterclaimed from them £900. They alleged that they had, after notice to him, sold some of the shares for which he had not paid and had thus incurred a loss – he denied this, but the basis for his counterclaim is not known. He started an action against them for the £900, and they responded by commencing an action against him. Thereupon he abandoned his claim. The stockbrokers made a complaint about his conduct to the Liverpool Stock Exchange and his name was posted in the Exchange on what was called "the Yellow Board", on which the names of defaulters appeared. According to Coleman, Edwin Jackson left Liverpool and went to live at Norton, but very soon afterwards he re-appeared at Coleman's office, dressed shabbily in a torn coat, and said he wanted to reach a settlement of the debt because his brother Ralph, of Hartlepool, had arranged a favourable opening for him if he could clear up his liabilities in Liverpool, and had lent him £200 or £300 to do this. He offered 2s. 6d. in the £ on Coleman's claim of £1,200 and a lump sum of £50, but Coleman would not, at that time, accept it. However, when Edwin wrote some time later saying that if Coleman would not accept it he would go bankrupt, Coleman, on the advice of his solicitors, did accept. A meeting took place between Coleman's partner, Todd, and Edwin's solicitor, John Stamper, and, Coleman says, a receipt, "written in a very small hand", had been prepared by Stamper and was signed by Todd in the name of the firm. Coleman's account of this is the first indication that he was not, perhaps, as straightforward and honest as he frequently claimed to be, because he refers to this receipt as though he did not know what was in it and implies that if he had known, he would not have signed it and that it was in any case unreadable. There seems no reason to doubt that both he and Todd knew that it was a legally-worded receipt in full and final settlement for all claims which the firm had against Edwin in respect of the alleged debt of £1,210. 12s. 6d.

It might be thought that that would have been the end of the matter and indeed so it seemed to be at the time, for Coleman said, "After this, no intercourse by letter or otherwise, ever took place between Mr. Jackson and myself until early in the year 1855" – i.e. nine years later.

In those intervening years Edwin had lived at Norton, apparently without occupation, but in 1854 he went to live at Bayswater in London, as he said, "for the education of my children". How he managed is not clear, but his wife had income under her marriage settlement. In London Edwin sought to establish himself in business in the City.

Coleman, too, after the failure of his business in Liverpool, had gone to London and, whilst living in Ealing, had an address or two in central London, where he sought to make a living by commercial activities, or perhaps by other means.

Walking about the City, as they did, Edwin and Coleman saw each other fairly often, but gave no acknowledgement of recognition. But in the spring of 1855 they did speak to each other. How that happened is not agreed by them – Edwin says Coleman stopped him in the street and asked him what he was doing in London. He followed this first encounter with several others and with letters in which he told Edwin that he was very hard up and begged for a loan of £350. According to Coleman, however, Edwin made the first approach and, after general remarks about their being in London, said that he was now occupying an influential position and would like to be of some service to Coleman, whereupon Coleman told him "the best service you can render me will be to pay me the balance of 1846". He acknowledges that they had further meetings, but says these were "to consult me", and that, during one of these meetings Edwin had said he was hoping to become a director of the new Bank which was being established under the name of "the London and Paris Bank", for which the firm of Cazenove & Co. were acting as brokers. Of these two versions, Edwin's seems preferable, because there was no dispute that a letter was written, in December, 1855, in which Coleman asked Edwin for a loan of £350.

Coleman was calling on Cazenove & Co. frequently and he also knew and had contact with Samuel Woods, a member of the London Stock Exchange who had, in 1845–46, been a member of the Liverpool Stock Exchange and thus knew about the posting of Edwin's name on the "Yellow Board". On the 21st of December, 1855, a momentous meeting took place which started by Edwin's and Coleman's travelling on the same horsedrawn bus from Bayswater into central London. Coleman called it "a singular accident". Whether or not it was that, it was certainly a singular coincidence that in Coleman's pocket there was a letter which he had received that very morning from Cazenove & Co., in which Coleman was asked whether he could give any information "about the character and respectability of Mr. Edwin Jackson, who is now a director of the London and Paris Bank. Mr. Samuel Woods (late of Liverpool and now in the London Stock Exchange) tells me that his conduct in certain transactions in produce, with several firms there, in 1846 or 1847, was such that he was compelled to vacate the town, with loss of character as well as money. Mr. Woods says he believes you yourself were one of the unfortunate sufferers". How, and why, this letter came to be in Coleman's pocket at that strategic moment is anybody's guess, but it served Coleman just as he wanted, for he said, "I put it into Mr. Jackson's hand and asked him – What reply should I make to it?" Edwin said he answered – "Answer it as you would any other letter, say what is just and true." But Coleman said that Edwin seemed much disconcerted and earnestly begged him to talk the matter over with him before answering it.

Whatever the exact words used, Coleman's account seems to fit in with what followed. He was on his way to a temporary office which he was using in Whitehall and Edwin accompanied him there and sat, for twenty minutes, in an outer office. There he scribbled some notes of what he would wish Coleman to say in reply to Cazenove's letter. Then the pair walked together up Whitehall and along the Strand and went into Simpson's Hotel, as it was then called. They took a private room and talked for an hour or two. What could have occupied them for all that time is puzzling, unless some rather difficult negotiations were taking place. According to Coleman, Edwin reiterated his wish to extinguish the balance of the original debt of £1,210 and, whilst he could not do so at once, promised to pay £150 in cash and, subsequently, by instalments, a further £500 on account, on condition that Coleman would write such a letter to Cazenove's as would uphold Edwin in his position as director of the Bank. According to Edwin, Coleman said he must answer the letter somehow and asked him to sketch out a suitable reply – which he did, as follows:

Disputed a/c which has been settled to my satisfaction. I believe he had hardly any other creditors. Not being in business, he left Liverpool to reside in Yorkshire; not from compulsion, as you state, or loss of character, and there he acquired a reputation to which the enclosed bear ample testimony, and he has others of a similar kind. I believe he is a man of high principle and of good connexions, and likely to be of service to your Bank

Coleman said he could not go as far as that, but he thought

he could frame a letter which would answer the purpose, and ultimately they agreed on this:

December 21st, 1855.

Dear Cazenove,

I beg in reply to your enquiries respecting Mr. Edwin Ward Jackson to say, that the late firm of Coleman and Todd had large transactions with him in 1845–6, which ended in a disputed account, and very angry feelings. Subsequently Mr. Jackson confessed his error, redeemed his credit, and I have nothing now to complain of.

After leaving Liverpool, he went, I believe, to reside in the neighbourhood of his Family in Yorkshire, who are highly respectable and influential.

I know from his Wife's trustees, that she had a considerable property settled upon her, which enables him to live out of business.

I saw, some time past, some paragraphs in the Yorkshire papers, highly complimentary to him, which leads me to the belief that he was there much esteemed.

I know him to be an intelligent and active man of business, and I have no doubt he will make a good Director of your Bank.

I am glad to hear that you have a good Subscription List.

Yours very truly,

BENJAMIN COLEMAN.

Edward Cazenove, Esq.

Coleman said he asked Edwin to put their agreement into writing, but Edwin objected but said he would bring him £150 in cash the next day and also a letter binding himself to the payment of a further £500. He urged Coleman to hurry back to his other office in the City so that he could write the letter and send it by hand to Cazenove's the same day, and before Edwin would next meet Cazenove. Coleman said there seemed no reason why he should not be given an I.O.U. for the £150 and that Edwin wrote one on a slip of paper and gave it to him. The next morning Edwin called on him and gave him the £150 for which he gave an ordinary receipt and handed back the I.O.U. He said Edwin excused himself from giving the letter promising the payment of the further £500, as he was "prevented from entering into written engagements". However, he (*Coleman*) might be assured it would be paid and must trust in Edwin's honour.

Edwin's version is different. He says he gave no I.O.U. – simply a slip of paper saying "I will call and bring you the £150 tomorrow". He didn't promise to give a letter about a further £500 – indeed such a letter was never mentioned. Coleman had, however, said something about further contingent liabilities of his, and had suggested a further loan, which Edwin had refused. He says he asked for a promissory note for the repayment of the £150, which was merely a loan. Coleman, he says, exhibited great temper, but said he would give Edwin a promissory note on the following Wednesday.

That night Coleman wrote to Edwin and says that he reminded him of the circumstances under which they had renewed their intercourse "and of the many promises he [*Edwin*] had voluntarily made to him during the last twelve months" and begged that he would keep faith when they met on Wednesday "and render any further discussion unnecessary". Coleman does not reproduce a copy of this letter, which seems suspicious, but he does set out Edwin's reply, written on Christmas Eve, 1855:

> CRAVEN HILL GARDENS, HYDE PARK,
> Monday Evening, Dec. 24th, 1855.

Sir,

I received this afternoon your very extraordinary letter, a production it would be as difficult to characterise as it would be to propound the fable which it contains.

And I acknowledge it simply to state, that I cannot now call upon you as I intended, on Wednesday morning, to receive from you your promissory note for the £150 I lent you without security, in cash last week, but request you to send me the same by return of post. Your letter, however, instructs me that it is not well to allow one's compassion to get the better of prudence and caution; and also teaches that it is not safe to allow oneself to be induced to help a man in his necessities.

I shall deem it necessary to take proper advice on the matter and manner of your letter.

E. WARD JACKSON.

To Mr. Benjamin Coleman

Coleman says the receipt of this letter aroused in his mind the strongest feelings of indignation and to this letter, and the attempt to enforce the repayment of the £150, must be attributed all that subsequently influenced his conduct.

Edwin commenced an action against Coleman for the recovery of the £150 and Coleman commenced an action against Edwin (presumably for the payment of the £500.) The two actions proceeded to the point to being heard, but then Edwin's solicitor announced that they wanted to withdraw and suggested a mutual release, Edwin to pay all costs. Coleman refused this but did settle for £150 plus his solicitor's costs (which, he said, amounted to £90.) A mutual release was made by a Judge's Order and Coleman admits that that put an end to any legal claim he had. He says, however, "but, whether rightly or wrongly, I thought my moral claims on Jackson to pay all he ever owed me, were not barred by this settlement – but, on the contrary, that they were stronger than ever".

It seems likely that what actually took place, during that meeting in Simpson's, was that Edwin agreed to pay £150 for the letter clearing him with Cazenove but that the £500 was not part of the bargain, or, indeed, mentioned. After all, why £500? Why not the balance of Coleman's original claim, which would have been about £860? Further, the letter which Coleman does not reproduce probably raised for the first time the suggestion that, if Edwin did not pay him more money, he would write again to Cazenove and undo the good which his first letter was expected to have achieved. This writing of letters by Coleman immediately after what seems to have been a settlement, is typical of a blackmailer and this would not be the only occasion when Coleman exhibited this tendency. Indeed he showed it again, and even more clearly, immediately after the Court settlement of the two claims had been made by the Judge's Order for on the very day of the settlement he wrote to the Rev. Mr. Plumer, Rector of Elstree, who, he had discovered, was a friend of the Ward Jackson family, and said that he would never rest until Edwin had fully redeemed the promises he had "frequently and solemnly made" and that "he did not think Mr. Ralph Jackson could be aware of the manner in which his brother, Edwin, had compromised the family name; so satisfied was he of the correctness of his conduct that he would gladly leave all questions in dispute to Mr. Ralph Jackson's sole adjudication, and on his decision bury everything in oblivion". This quotation (and those on preceding pages) has been taken from the pamphlet, *Extraordinary Case of Libel*, published by Coleman in June, 1858, and what follows it is worth remembering in relation to the attacks which Coleman made against Ralph Ward Jackson and which are described in later pages. He said – "Mr. Ralph Jackson was an entire stranger to me, and I had evidently miscalculated on his care about his brother's reputation; for, although my letter was shown to him by Mr. Plumer, he unfortunately took no notice of my offer, and thus the opportunity was lost of putting an end to disputes that have led to all the consequences which have followed." The consequences which had followed by June, 1858 were nothing to the consequences that followed after that date. Perhaps the latter were not consequences at all but arose from quite different impulses. The reader must make his own judgment when he has read the whole story.

The failure to get Ralph directly into negotiation with him did not deter Coleman from pursuing Edwin. Rooting around, he learned, some six months later, that Edwin had been appointed a magistrate for Middlesex and so he sent a letter to Edwin telling him, in effect, that unless he paid-up, he, Coleman, would start writing to Edwin's fellow magistrates and "would never allow him to hold up his head amongst these gentlemen." Edwin put that letter in the hands of his solicitors and they immediately wrote to Coleman saying that it could only be regarded as an audacious attempt to extort money and, if there was any more of it, it would meet with summary punishment. Nothing daunted, Coleman wrote to Edwin threatening to go to Liverpool to see John Campbell, who was Edwin's wife's trustee in her marriage settlement and therefore a man of great importance to Edwin. One gets the impression that relations between Edwin and Campbell were not as warm as they might have been. Coleman also threatened that he would write to the Home Secretary, Sir George Grey (who had supervisory functions in relation to magistrates' courts).

These threats producing no results, Coleman did go to Liverpool and told his story to John Campbell, who suggested that the dispute should be put to an arbitrator and wrote a letter to this effect, which he handed to Coleman. On the 1st of October, 1857, Coleman sent a copy of Campbell's letter to Edwin and said he was quite ready to refer the dispute to third parties and, for this purpose would be ready to meet Edwin on the 5th of October. Coleman's contact with Campbell worried Edwin enough for him to go to Liverpool where he tried to see Campbell, but failed. He was staying with one of his other brothers at 18, Colquitt Street, and from there he wrote a letter to Campbell which was to have momentous consequences:

(Private)
18, Colquitt Street,
6th, October, 1857.

My Dear Sir,

I regret very much I did not see you when I called yesterday afternoon. I did not wait, nor would I disturb you, as your clerk mentioned you were very particularly engaged.

But let me warn you about a certain individual – the most ungrateful of scoundrels – who is known to the magistrates and police of London, and equally well known to others as a panderer and a pimp, following as a vocation the trapping of the unwary, and pursuing every device for extorting money; any one whatever, be he who he may, that holds communication with him, will be drawn into a correspondence, and be surely entrapped in the end, and he will be lucky if he escapes being dragged into a Court of

Law in contest with a man whose social standing is among the reptiles of our species.

Of course I should court arbitration where such a course was proper, and the party not a villian; but let me simply state, that all accounts have been fully and finally settled, and that every sentence and circumstance contained in a certain letter (of which I lately received a copy) is a fabrication or distortion, and forms part of a network or plot, having for the object intimidation, and in the end, money extortion. My brother magistrates in Middlesex are fully acquainted with his goings on, and recommend me contemptuous silence.

This man made confession and amends to me years ago for his conduct towards me at that time, when the accounts were mutually and satisfactorily settled. He crawled before me lately, and on repeated entreaty, received pecuniary assistance. By trumping up fabulous statements, and by utterly distorting facts and circumstances, he now seeks occasion to extort money by vain and futile threats, which, to any one versed in the world's ways, must be too transparent not to be seen through, and which, of course, I cast to the winds.

I request you will be so good as to treat this letter as private and confidential, except to Mr. John Turner.

And I remain, my dear Sir,

Your's very truly,

E. WARD JACKSON

Coleman, after seeing Campbell, had gone to Paris, for a reason that he does not define, but possibly to get some information about the London and Paris Bank and to see how he could damage Edwin in his position in it. When he returned to London he says he found, in an envelope addressed to him, but with a slip of paper inside which suggested that it had originally gone to a third party who held an important position in the London Stock Exchange, the following anonymous letter, written, he says, in the hand of a lawyer's clerk:

Sir, – There is a deep-dyed scoundrel about town who has tried various dodges for the purpose of extorting money. His practice is to scrape acquaintance with gentlemen, as with myself, and others, and get to know their history, and then, by trumped up tales, simulated reports, and perverted statements, to threaten to expose them. I understand he has been lately trying his hand with two gentlemen, one a member of the Stock Exchange, and the other a respectable merchant, but has failed, both of which have come to my knowledge under circumstances which leave no doubt of their truth. Other cases are mentioned, for which, however, I cannot vouch. Having heard him boast of you among his personal friends, I deem it a duty to a man occupying your position to write and caution you to be on your guard against the advances of this designing, plausible Jew, whom I have discovered to be a most cunning, unscrupulous man, and whose vocation in the city seems to be to trip up the unguarded and ensnare his benefactors. His name is Coleman.

Yours &c.,

A CITY MERCHANT.

City, Oct. 17th.

P.S. – I obviously cannot give you my name in a letter by post, but will give particulars when I see you.

Coleman says that he at once knew that the author must have been Edwin, so he instructed his solicitor to apply for a summons for criminal libel. This application was made on the 30th October, 1857, at the Mansion House Magistrates' Court, but was refused. Edwin was represented by a barrister – Serjeant Parry – who said this was part of an abominable scheme by Coleman to extort money and, therefore, he asked for Coleman to be taken into custody and charged accordingly. The magistrate said he could not do that and if they wanted to prosecute him they would have to apply for a summons in the usual way. Four days later they did apply but, like Coleman's, their application was refused for want of prima facie evidence.

On the 6th of November, 1857, a letter from Edwin appeared in *The Times* and, in it, he made an emphatic denial that he had had anything to do with the alleged libel – "I had no hand whatever in writing or publishing it and I never saw or heard of it until I received the summons."

This publicity had an unfortunate result for Edwin because William Dredge, a Civil Engineer with whom Coleman had some dealings, sent Coleman a letter which he had received and which was in identical terms with those in the anonymous defamatory letter. In Coleman's opinion it was undoubtedly in Edwin's handwriting. He then made an attempt, through his solicitors, to arrange a meeting with Edwin's solicitors "to enable them to advise their client with more or less confidence". They didn't respond so he made another application for a summons for defamation, this time at the Westminster Magistrates' Court, and it was granted.

And now, for the first time, Ralph Ward Jackson took an obvious and direct part in trying to protect his brother, for he turned up at the hearing of the summons as one of five witnesses who swore that the letter written to Dredge was not in Edwin's handwriting. The magistrate dismissed the summons. Coleman adds spice to his account of these proceedings by suggesting that there was an attempt by Edwin's solicitors to steal the defamatory letter written to Dredge as it was being passed about in the Court.

Coleman, in addition to his other characteristics, undoubtedly possessed a perseverance which vied with that of Ralph's in his pursuit of the Rev. Burges, for he next decided to try his hand at a civil action for damages for the alleged libel and, after issuing a writ, he asked the other side to refer the matter to arbitration. They indignantly refused.

But now he received more ammunition by getting hold of a letter, of similar defamatory character, which had been sent to James Hutchinson, Chairman of the Stock Exchange, and he heard that similar letters had been sent to two Middlesex magistrates. Always preferring negotiation to direct legal action, he again tried to frighten Edwin by saying that he was again going to Liverpool to tell John Campbell all about it. Edwin tried to forestall him by instructing his solicitors to write to Campbell informing him of the two unsuccessful attempts at criminal prosecution and suggesting the inexpediency of his seeing Coleman, as "his only motive is to prejudice your mind and, if possible, to secure your attendance at the approaching trial at Westminster".

However, Campbell did see Coleman on the 11th of January, 1858 and, to Coleman's surprise and delight, showed him the letter he had received from Edwin's solicitors and also the "private" letter which Edwin had written to him on the 6th of October. This was convincing evidence that Edwin had been writing defamatory letters. Campbell was also good enough to show Coleman the reply which he was about to send to Edwin's solicitors, in which he said he was reluctant to be mixed-up in the dispute, but that he was satisfied that the anonymous letters had been written by Edwin. This undoubtedly alarmed Edwin and his advisers and not only his solicitor, Mr. Jarvis, but also Ralph, made visits to Liverpool to try to persuade Campbell to change his view. Coleman knew of these visits because his step-son had an office a few doors away from Campbell's and was acting as an informer and go-between. Campbell had an aversion to being dragged into any Court hearing and he asked, through Coleman's step-son, what terms Coleman would accept to put an end to the whole disagreeable affair. Coleman replied that his chief object was to be completely exonerated and justified, which might be done in a letter for publication which need not necessarily admit Edwin's guilt "and as to compensation, I would leave that part of the question entirely to Mr. Campbell's discretion."

Campbell said he would be pleased to act as a conciliator, but Edwin or his brothers would have to ask him to do so. No such request was forthcoming, so Coleman wrote another long letter to Campbell on the 30th of January, 1858, in which he emphasised the strength of the evidence he now possessed and hinted that, in addition to the pending civil action, he might try another criminal prosecution, by indictment at the Old Bailey.

No conciliation took place and the civil action was set down for trial in the Court of Queen's Bench on the 20th of February, 1858. Coleman had a Q.C. and a Junior. Edwin had two Q.Cs. and a Junior, and, in addition to his solicitor, Jarvis, Ralph, who was a solicitor, was present, advising and helping. According to Coleman he took a leading part in the negotiations which took place immediately before the case was called, and which resulted in an agreement to refer the case to arbitration instead of its being heard and determined in Court. According to Coleman, the approach for this came from Edwin's side and it is easy to believe that they may have wished to avoid the publicity that would have resulted from a public hearing. But they were outmanoeuvred by Coleman, who imposed conditions on the reference to an arbitrator which gave him the possibility of much more than he could have expected from a Court's decision. He insisted, and Edwin's side agreed, that the balance of the original debt should be an open question and not barred by the Statute of Limitations, nor by the Judge's Order in the 1855 actions, nor by the receipt which had been given in 1846 when Coleman's claim was first settled. He also insisted on being given £150 immediately, but as a matter of account, pending the decision. Perhaps Ralph, who was now getting deeply involved in this tiresome dispute of his brother's, thought it was a small price to pay to avoid the publicity of a Court hearing. A few hundred pounds, though a lot of money to ordinary men in those days, was of little significance to the man who was spending millions in building his port and town of West Hartlepool. If he did think so, he underestimated the propensities of this dreadful man with whom his brother had become so embarrassingly entangled.

Three arbitrators were appointed – one by Edwin's side, one by Coleman's and the third to be agreed upon by these two arbitrators or, failing agreement, to be appointed by the Solicitor-General. Edwin's arbitrator was T. Pope, who was Ralph's London agent for coal shipments from West Hartlepool. Coleman's was William Warnes, one of his City friends. There was no agreement as to who should be the third arbitrator so an application had to be made to the Solicitor-General and Coleman complained that although that would normally have been a formality taken in Chambers, Ralph turned up with a barrister who had been a junior to the Solicitor-General when he, acting as a barrister, had been retained by Ralph in a Chancery suit concerning Christ Church.

The Solicitor-General appointed William Elmsley, Q.C. Before the arbitration commenced Coleman tried his hand with Ralph once more. He asked for an interview and, when this was arranged in London, told Ralph that he had come to him "in the fullness of his strength". He produced John Campbell's letter and tried to get Ralph to read a copy of Edwin's letter to Campbell. Ralph said he wouldn't look at any letters that were not originals. Coleman taunted him that he dare not read it, but Ralph still refused and then "he asked me with great calmness and suavity of manner, what was the practical object of my visit". Coleman told him he would be satisfied with a letter absolving him from the imputations which had been made on his character and conduct, and a substantial sum as compensation for the libels. He would not ask for an admission of his brother's guilt but would leave the world to find out the real character of Edwin. He would hand over all the documents in his possession to be destroyed. Ralph answered – "You have mixed me up with my brother. You must know that I have nothing to do with him. If he has done wrong, he must take the consequences." Coleman replied that he was surprised, and sorry he had taken the trouble to arrange the meeting. "I said his words were quite irreconcileable with his acts, seeing that he had stood by his brother throughout this inquiry in a manner not even justified by the ties of kindred. I left him, declaring this was the last opportunity he should ever have of saving his brother from the disgrace that undoubtedly awaited him."

The arbitration commenced on the 16th of March, 1858. Counsel appeared for both sides – one barrister for Coleman, a Q.C. and a junior for Edwin – and again Ralph was there, both as a witness and as a solicitor helping Jarvis. Evidence was taken on oath and Ralph swore that the letters to Dredge and Hutchinson were not in Edwin's handwriting but that he thought they were a good imitation. Other witnesses for Edwin were a Mr. Atkins and a Mr. Thomas Winkworth (who was an important man in the City and a director of the Commercial Bank). For Coleman the witnesses were Dredge and Hutchinson – to prove receipt of the letters – but Hutchinson, on being pressed, said he believed Edwin was the writer of both letters. John Campbell gave evidence of the letter written to him by Edwin on the 6th of October, 1857 and said he believed both the anonymous letters were in the hand of Edwin. A most damaging witness against Edwin was James Kemp, who had been an acquaintance of his and who said he had advised Edwin not to write the anonymous letters and also that Edwin had tried to deceive him about his handwriting by sending him a note written in a grotesquely large hand. Three other witnesses who swore they knew Edwin's writing gave their opinion that the defamatory letters were his, and two handwriting experts gave similar opinions. Perhaps the most damning thing that happened was that, when Edwin's case opened, the other side asked for the witnesses to be excluded from the room, except when they were giving their evidence, and, for the purpose of cross-examining them, Coleman's Counsel showed them several specimens of writing – some of which were acknowledged to be Edwin's, and others, undoubtedly not. Edwin's first witness, Atkins, having made a mess of this test, Edwin was seen to leave the room and then quickly return before Thomas Winkworth was called. As soon as he re-entered the room Coleman's Counsel asked him whether he had spoken to Winkworth, and he firmly and repeatedly denied that he had. But when Winkworth was asked whether Edwin had spoken to him he admitted that he had, and had tried to forewarn him about the handwriting test. This completely took the wind out of Edwin's Counsel and he, in effect, gave up the case.

On the 29th of April, 1858, the Arbitrators announced their Award and, by a majority of two to one, found Edwin guilty of writing the anonymous letters to Dredge and Hutchinson and awarded Coleman £400 damages and his costs. They also ordered Edwin to pay the arbitration fees of £480.

Coleman's account of this affair ends with words that have

Architect's drawing of the Swainson Dock Warehouse.

J. W. Carmichael's painting of West Hartlepool in 1859 as seen from the tower of Christ Church. (This painting originally belonged to Ralph Ward Jackson and was presented by his son to the West Hartlepool Improvement Commissioners in 1882.)

an ominous ring for Ralph Ward Jackson. After reporting that at the end of the Arbitration Edwin's Counsel had said, "Mr. Ralph Ward Jackson is desirous that I should mention that he is not supporting his brother in this case" (meaning, not supporting the defence financially), he writes, "Against this assertion made at the request of Mr. Ralph Jackson, I must enter my most earnest protest". Then he lists his complaints against Ralph:

> It was Mr. Ralph Ward Jackson who came to the Westminster police court, attended by his family solicitor and a *protégé* of his own, to swear the anonymous letter sent to Mr. Dredge was not his brother's writing, "and nothing like it."
>
> It was Mr. Ralph Ward Jackson who went twice to Liverpool, after Mr. Jarvis had been there, *and with a knowledge of the existence of the fatal letter of the 6th of October*, to dissuade Mr. Campbell from supporting me.
>
> It was Mr. Ralph Ward Jackson who negociated the terms of the arbitration.
>
> It was Mr. Ralph Ward Jackson who nominated his own agent as his brother's arbitrator!
>
> It was Mr. Ralph Ward Jackson who caused an unnecessary delay in fixing on the third arbitrator.
>
> It was Mr. Ralph Ward Jackson who went, accompanied by a friend of the Solicitor-General, to that gentleman's chambers, to ask for the nomination of the third arbitrator!
>
> It was Mr. Ralph Ward Jackson who claimed the privilege of remaining as his brother's adviser in the presence of the arbitrators when all the other witnesses were requested to leave the room.
>
> And finally it was Mr. Ralph Ward Jackson who in the face of the evidence I have here recorded presented himself as the last witness and, for the second time, swore the anonymous letters were not his brother's writing, "But they were a good imitation!"
>
> It is therefore worse than folly for Mr. Ralph Ward Jackson to try at this late period to free himself from whatever amount of

responsibility may attach to him for the conspicuous exertions
he has used to defeat the proofs I brought in support of the charge
I originally made, that his brother was the author and writer of
the anonymous letters.

The first sickening indication to the Jacksons that their
enemy was still after them was the publication of the pamphlet
– *Extraordinary Case of Libel* – previously mentioned. This
came within two months of the Arbitration Award, and the
pamphlet was addressed to the Members of the Stock
Exchange, the Magistrates of the County of Middlesex and
the Commercial Community generally. It was priced 1s. and
declared itself "to be had of all booksellers". Coleman tried
to justify the publication by saying "it was the only means
I had of making the result known" and alleged "it was eagerly
bought up in the Northern districts and a number of letters
were addressed to me by entire strangers, complimenting me
on my energy and congratulating me on the result". He denied
that he ever distributed a single copy to any member of the
Jackson family or to any one else in the Counties of Durham
or Yorkshire. Ralph, however, said that he published and
circulated it among his relatives, friends and neighbours and
disturbed the peace of mind of his aged mother, his brother's
wife and other members of the family.

If the motive of the Jacksons in seeking arbitration had been
to avoid publicity, they had badly miscalculated. Having
exposed themselves to the whole of Coleman's original claim
being re-opened, they lost both ways, for there can be little
doubt that Coleman saw to it that the pamphlet reached every-
body who might wish to harm the Jacksons, and particularly
Ralph, who had now become his principal quarry.

And, not content with the publicity, Coleman, in spite of
the receipt given in 1846, the settlement of 1855, the arbitration
of 1858, continued his demands for more money. Let him try
to justify himself:

Some time after [*i.e. the publication of the pamphlet*] I wrote to
Mr. Ralph Jackson, reminding him that the old balance of £710

was still due to me in honour, and though I had no legal claim for its payment, I thought my moral claim was stronger than ever; made so, by the course which had been pursued by him and his brother; and that as I had Mr. Edwin Jackson at my mercy by his having been convicted of perjury before the arbitrators, I would never remain satisfied until his debt was fully discharged. Mr. Jackson took no notice of my letter. *Two or three months after-wards* I made a visit to the North, when I called on many persons, and heard such a character of Mr. Ralph Ward Jackson, as satisfied me that the extraordinary and dishonest course of conduct pursued by him in his brother's case was precisely what might have been expected from his known antecedents. It is impossible, I assure you, to exaggerate the statements made to me of his cruel heartlessness and double dealing in various ways, and particularly in the matter of the Christ Church affair, where, under the cloak of religion, he did acts which stamp his name with infamy – Acts which so aroused the indignation of the humble people in defence of their pastor, who was struck on the steps of the church by his would-be master, Mr. Ralph Jackson, that his reign at West Hartlepool had well nigh been brought to a speedy termination. The facts are on record. They are published in a pamphlet, and you who desire to estimate the real character of a man who is now held up by ignorant or interested partizans as entitled to your gratitude 'for the unselfishness and high honour which have always characterized his conduct', will no doubt look to it. I then heard of various things connected with his policy and conduct in the management of your affairs [*i.e. the shareholders' affairs*] which assured me there was ample room for enquiry into what, as I afterwards found, Mr. George Bidder the eminent engineer had described before a Committee of the House of Commons as something 'very rotten in the state of Denmark', and I determined to investigate it for myself.

Having heard that Coleman was trying to acquire a small amount of stock in his Company, Ralph Jackson smelt danger and, on the 8th of October, 1858, wrote to Coleman's friend and arbitrator, William Warne, and offered to try to bring about a final settlement of the dispute between Coleman and Edwin. After considerable correspondence the £710 claimed by Coleman as the balance "due to him in honour" was paid

and Ralph, with the caution of a solicitor, drew up a receipt
for signature by Coleman, the terms of which, he hoped, would
close the door on any further demands or claims:

> I, BENJAMIN COLEMAN, late of Liverpool, and now of 28, Thread-
> needle-Street, London, hereby acknowledge that Edwin Ward
> Jackson, esquire, of 14, Craven Hill Gardens, Bayswater, London,
> has this day advanced and paid me the sum of Seven hundred
> and ten pounds, which I allege and declare to have been previously
> discharged at Law, and to be solely and only now remaining a
> debt of honour from him to me – being the last and sole remnant,
> but due merely in honour – in respect of all transactions, dealings,
> accounts, litigation and proceedings whatsoever which have ever
> occurred, existed, or passed between him and myself, whether
> solely or jointly; and, on thus receiving from the said Edwin Ward
> Jackson, in honour, the above sum of Seven hundred and ten
> pounds, I unfeignedly admit and declare that he has fully and
> honourably satisfied me, as well in law as in honour, and on every
> other ground, for and in respect of every account, promise, claim
> and complaint whatsoever; and that, for effecting this honourable
> and final arrangement, and my receiving the above sum, I am
> wholly indebted to the kind and honourable consideration of his
> mother, as I am informed, his brother, Ralph Ward Jackson,
> esquire, and their family, assisted by my friend, William Warne,
> esquire, of Tottenham, Middlesex.
>
> Witness my hand this Tenth day of December, One thousand
> eight hundred and fifty-eight.
>
> BENJ. COLEMAN
>
> Witness to the signing hereof by the above-named
> Benjamin Coleman,
>
> WM. WARNE, Tottenham, N.

The money paid, and the receipt, in these cast-iron terms,
signed and witnessed, Ralph was surely entitled to think he
had heard the last of Coleman? Imagine, therefore, the chilling
misery he must have felt when the post arrived at his office
on the morning of the 17th of December, 1858 – just one week
after the signing of the receipt and one week before Christmas.
The, by now, familiar envelope and handwriting, and, inside,
this:

To Ralph Ward Jackson, Esq., West Hartlepool.
London, 16th December 1858,
28, Threadneedle-street.

Sir,

Recent events will doubtless have prepared you for a communication from me, and although I would gladly have avoided all further correspondence with you, placing you in the same position as I now feel bound to regard your brother Edwin, by drawing a veil over the past, no longer permitting myself to dwell on wrongs which have embittered the domestic peace of myself and family for many months past, yet I am unable to do so, and this inability, I am relieved to think arises from your own course of conduct.

The determined manner in which you have rejected overtures made by me at various times to enable you to form a just appreciation of my character, and the nature of my transactions with your brother Edwin, destroyed all idea of a good understanding being established between us.

My last effort in that direction was expressed in my letter to you of the 31st of July in the present year, written, I confess, in the spirit of forlorn hope, but consonant with the principle I had adopted throughout the unhappy struggle in which I had been so long engaged. From some cause this letter did at length awaken you to the propriety of inducing your brother to pay a debt from which he was legally absolved, and thus to satisfy the only remaining claim I had made upon him; but unfortunately you delayed your mediation too long; I had waited for the possible recognition of this letter for *two months*! and influenced by my previous experience, no letter of mine *nor act of conciliation having ever been acknowledged by you before*, without a hope of its producing a favourable result, I was induced at the latter end of September to make a journey into the counties of Durham and Lancaster to see some of the many persons who, after the perusal of my pamphlet, had written me complimentary and sympathising letters, and I found your recent conduct to me was only what might have been expected from the character of other transactions in which you had been unenviably conspicuous, and of which I had indisputable evidence.

Smarting under a sense of the great injustice I had suffered, you can hardly feel surprised that I should be ready, under the circumstances, to take advantage of what appeared to me a legitimate opportunity of showing up the real character of a man who had done all he could to blast my reputation and the happiness of my wife and family. Hence my present position of antagonism to you.

Coleman had, in fact, now become a small shareholder in the West Hartlepool Harbour and Railway Company. No more money was to be had from the Jacksons but perhaps there would be other sources?

The Coleman Attack

With the ownership of the small amount of stock which he had acquired, Coleman was legally entitled to attend the general meetings of the West Hartlepool Harbour and Railway Company, and he lost no time in preparing the attack which he would deliver at the next Annual General Meeting to be held in West Hartlepool on the 26th of February, 1859. To canvass support he sent printed circulars to the share and debenture holders on the 12th and 24th of January, calling their attention "to the necessity of enquiring into the past administration and present financial position" of the Company. How much he then knew about the irregularities is uncertain, but it would seem that he knew that steamships and collieries were being subsidised by the Company's funds; that the capital of the Company was not truly stated; that some bonds, for large amounts, had been issued without legal authority; that some debentures had been hurriedly repaid by the Chairman when their value had been questioned; and that the accounts of the Company were likely to have been improperly kept.

Ralph Ward Jackson tried to counter his impending attack by sending his own circular to the shareholders on the 18th of January and, in it, giving his own account of the steps he had taken to try to settle the dispute between Edwin Ward Jackson and Coleman and letting them see the terms of the receipt which Coleman had given for the final payment of £710.

Coleman says (and it was never denied) that the walls of West Hartlepool were, shortly before the date of the annual meeting, placarded with bills which read:

£100 REWARD

WHEREAS, a certain ADVENTURER, by name

COLEMAN

Has, by the publication of a series of Letters, Libelling the
character of Ralph Ward Jackson, Esq., as Chairman of the
West Hartlepool Dock and Railway Company, and thus
endeavoured to cause a breach of confidence in that Gentleman on the part of the Shareholders, which would have a
tendency to create a Panic in this Town that would be attended
with the most disastrous results to every Inhabitant,

NOW, this is to give NOTICE

That the said Benjamin Coleman will be at West Hartlepool
on Friday, the 25th instant, and that the above reward will
be given to any person who shall produce the body of the said
B. Coleman

DEAD OR ALIVE!

West Hartlepool, February 17th, 1859.

Whether Coleman knew of this incitement before he came to
the town is not known, but he did face an annual meeting in
which he found no supporters but many critics. Nevertheless
he persisted in his allegation that there was something very
seriously wrong in the accounts and affairs of the company
which needed investigation. The Directors evidently thought
that the best way of handling him was to appoint a "Committee
of Assistance", and to arrange the membership of it so as to
ensure, as far as possible, that its findings would not be
injurious to the Company. Coleman says it was hand-picked
by the Chairman. It consisted of Admiral Cator and Messrs.
Sturge, Birley, Wood, and Baynes.

Later, Coleman would criticise the composition of the Committee, but, for the moment, he appeared to be satisfied that
the chairman of it, Thomas Sturge, was a man of the highest

reputation in the commercial world, a wealthy Quaker with long experience of railway undertakings. Moreover, he had, before the meeting finished, come to Coleman's side and whispered in his ear that he would like to visit him in London and hear the details of his complaints about the Company's management. Coleman says that Sturge visited him twice and that altogether they spent eight hours in each other's company, during which Coleman gave a written account of his allegations. Sturge had assured him that he knew all about West Hartlepool, but would investigate the complaints "to the bottom". He had added – "You must not say nor write another word at present; wait until I have made myself master of the case. It will take some time; you must not be too anxious."

But as the weeks and months rolled on, and Coleman heard nothing, he did become anxious and irritated. However he received great encouragement and help from a pamphlet – *The Past and Present Financial and Commercial Position of the West Hartlepool Harbour and Railway Company considered* – which was, in the middle of 1859, published by a City firm, Baily Brothers of the Royal Exchange Buildings (price 6d.). It analysed the Company's published accounts for 1855, 1856, 1857 and 1858, and criticised their inaccuracy, particularly in relation to the statements of the Company's share and loan capital, the wide discrepancy between the figures for the merchandise exports and the revenue earned from that traffic, and the apparent payment of dividends out of capital. It also revealed some detailed information about the ownership of the steamboats and collieries which were providing so large a part of the traffic.

Whether this firm were acting in collaboration with Coleman is not known. They said they "had held no communication on the subject of their paper with either the directors or the discontented shareholders". (In 1860 they published a second and revised edition of their pamphlet which was more critical of the direction of the Company and had more of the flavour of the Coleman pamphlets and circulars, but it may be that this was because Coleman used their information and copied their style.)

Between the 5th of July and the 26th of October, 1859, Coleman wrote to Sturge five times, enquiring what progress was being made and whether Sturge had not arrived at a stage where he could say that Coleman's allegations were justified. He got no satisfaction. Nor did he get any reply directly from Sturge – all were written by his secretaries and merely urged patience. By the 23rd of October Coleman was expressing his irritation – "It is now *eight* months since I placed in your hands the data upon which my charges against the management of the West Dock Company are founded and for that period I have, at your request, remained perfectly quiescent. I hope, therefore, that you will not consider it premature, nor unreasonable, if I should now press to be informed – confidentially, if you deem it necessary – of the result of your investigations and your view for the future." Sturge offered an interview, which took place on the 5th of November, but Coleman got no more assurance than that the delay was caused by the necessity of completing the transfer of some property from Jackson to the Company, that the report was nearly finished and that Sturge was about to call a meeting of the Committee of Assistance, in order to lay it before them for their approval.

Coleman wrote three more letters to Sturge and in the last, dated the 14th of December, he said he had put his case in the hands of solicitors, Yarborough and Wilkinson, and he urged Sturge to call on them. This brought a long reply, dated the 19th December, signed by Sturge's secretary, George Enderby, and it convinced Coleman that his trust in Sturge had been misplaced. Here are extracts:

> In reference to your letter of the 14th instant Mr. Sturge desires me to say that he has very carefully considered it. He is pleased to learn by it that you have placed yourself in the hands of Yarborough and Wilkinson, of 44, Lincoln-inn Fields, who, he has no doubt, will advise you discreetly.
>
> Mr. Struge thinks it would be altogether out of place for him

to wait upon them ... for (among other reasons) should their advice in any respect not meet your views, you might think they had been unduly influenced by him, and because he has nothing whatever to do with your private affairs.

Mr. Sturge only knows you as a shareholder of the West Hartlepool Harbour and Railway, who has avowed that he has no object in view but the success and prosperity of that undertaking. Mr. Sturge's labours are for the same end, and he will continue to pursue that object to the best of his ability....

At the proper time the report of the committee will (Mr. Sturge does not doubt) be published in its entirety. Mr. Struge thinks there is no justice in the remarks contained in your letter respecting anything which has been said by him to you ... You say, "You must see that I, at least, made a bad bargain in accepting the terms which have kept me silent for ten months". Mr. Sturge entirely denies the existence of any terms or bargain. What he did say was only to advise you that it would be better for your own standing to await with patience until the report of the committee should appear, and he thinks so still.

The final paragraphs must have infuriated Coleman:

Mr. Sturge can feel for the suffering you endure from the distracting power of impatience, for he himself is open to the same temptation of the evil one. That it is evil, may be seen in the 2nd. Peter, 1st. chap., 6th. verse, and in Isaiah, 26th chap., 3rd. verse is shewn that peace of mind which results from patience, spoken of by Peter, and how it is to be obtained.

To Mr. Sturge it will be a source of great pleasure should what is written be in any degree helpful towards restoring peace to your mind.

That letter did not finish the correspondence, but from then onwards the tone was cool and unfriendly.

The report was, in fact, finished by the 20th of December, and was then handed to the Company's directors, but not to Coleman. There was evidence that it had been leaked to the *Railway Times*, who, at the end of December, published an article condemning Coleman and praising the directors. It was not made available to the shareholders until immediately before the Annual General Meeting on the 23rd of February, 1860. Considering that it had taken nine months to prepare and the seriousness of the matters mentioned in it, it was much shorter than could be described as "commendably brief":

TO THE DIRECTORS OF THE WEST HARTLEPOOL HARBOUR AND
RAILWAY COMPANY.

The Committee of Assistance, appointed by the General Meeting of the Company, held on the 25th of February, 1859, report as follows:–

The Committee have to acknowledge that they have received from the Directors and Officers of the Company, every information and explanation which they required, and the Committee believe that the whole of the moneys raised by the Company have been applied to promote the interest of the Company, and that the works of the Company have been carried out ably with a due regard to economy. On considering the past, as well as the present position of the Company, the Committee have come to the conclusion that there have been errors of judgement on the part of the Directors, owing to their having entertained too sanguine a view of the rapidity with which the income of the Company's undertaking would increase. At the same time the Committee are themselves satisfied that there are good grounds for believing that the profits will steadily increase, – and it is only right that they should say, that, but for the *stimulus* of the sanguine view of the Company's prospects, under which the Directors have worked, they might not have exerted themselves as energetically as they have done in providing for the future extension of the Company's business.

While the Committee have formed their opinion of the future increase of the prosperity of the Company on what appears to them reliable grounds, yet they wish to be cautious against leading any to expect that such prosperity will be more rapid than the ordinary increase of mercantile advancement.

The Directors, on the other hand, appear to the Committee to be still very sanguine as to the earlier results. They may be right, – and it is for them to explain the grounds on which their views are based, that the shareholders may form their own conclusion thereon. Here the Committee would remark that, ample as the dock and warehouse accommodation is for the present, and even a greatly increased, trade, yet they think it would be a want of foresight to part with the land, not build on contiguous to the docks; and that such land ought to be reserved for their extension, as the increased trade of the port may require an enlargement of the docks, and other requisite dock accommodation.

The Committee now proceed to give their views upon the future prospects of the undertaking, which are now the most important subjects for consideration.

The Company have a valuable landed property – and, although the whole of it is not at present in use, a small portion of it only can be regarded as superfluous, – several acres a year are raised to a proper height with ballast, and then become saleable, realising to the Comapny, while being raised, a considerable profit as ballast deposit ground, and selling, when so improved, on terms very advantageous to the Company.

The Directors, mainly in the infancy of the undertaking, deemed it necessary to assist certain collieries on their lines of railway, in order to secure the large revenue arising from the traffic from those collieries. Although this assistance has been large, yet the Committee believe that the collieries afford an adequate security for payment of the interest, and ultimate repayment of the principal of the money so advanced.

The Company are also interested in steam vessels, which, though they may at first be advantageous to a company establishing a new seaport, yet, as they have not hitherto obtained special powers in respect to them, the Committee recommend that, in the absence of such powers, such arrangements be made as shall free the Company from any liability arising from their being interested in ships, or as carriers by sea.

The Company's preferential and share capital and liabilities exceed together, by about £500,000, the Parliamentary powers of the Company; but on a very cautious estimate of the value of the landed property, the securities on the collieries, and the steam vessels, the Committee are of opinion that their present value exceeds that amount, and that their prospective value is much greater. It is proposed by the bill which the Committee will presently refer to, to increase the capital to that extent.

The Company have given notice of an application to Parliament for regulating their capital and debt. The Committee have a bill prepared (a copy of which accompanies this report); and inasmuch as the provisions of the bill show the course which the Committee consider to be proper for placing the Company's affairs on a sound basis, the Committee feel that they may be excused for not encumbering this report with further details; and they recommend the Directors to adopt the same, and proceed to get it passed into a law in the next session of Parliament.

Mr. Benjamin Coleman, at the General Meeting of the Company, held on the 25th of February, 1859, having disavowed being actuated by any improper motives for the course which he took in drawing the attention of the shareholders to the state of the Company's affairs, the Committee consider that the shareholders are indebted to him for having called their particular attention to the position of the Company with a view to its improvement.

THOMAS STURGE, Chairman.

Northfleet, 20th, 12th Month, 1859.

If the left-handed compliment contained in the last paragraph of the report was intended to placate Coleman, it did nothing of the sort. The report was quite unsatisfactory to him, as, indeed, it was likely to have been, for his and Sturge's objects were really diametrically opposed. Coleman, though he would have denied it, wished to bring Jackson and the Company to a standstill; Sturge wanted to preserve the Company and assist it to continue with increased prosperity.

Jackson, armed in advance with the contents of the report, and in the comforting knowledge that it absolved him and his co-directors from any real blame, rallied all his supporters to attend the Annual Meeting to be held in West Hartlepool and to combine in squashing Coleman. The Directors' report to the meeting was self-laudatory, without reticence or trace of embarrassment, and contained a detailed recital of the amazing growth of traffic and revenue which was claimed to be the direct result of the Directors' activities. For the first time the now familiar claim was made that, in 1859, the value of merchandise foreign exports, had reached the astonishing value of £4,214,783. The Company's surplus lands (on which

West Hartlepool was being built) were it was said, becoming annually of increasing value over the original cost, and in demand for building and commercial purposes at high prices. A glowing prospect was painted of a large Harbour of Refuge being constructed in the Bay "by the aid of a million pounds sterling of public money". The Cleveland Railway, which had been formed to open out "a vast extent of newly discovered Ironstone Royalties", and in which the West Hartlepool Company had invested £60,000, would soon be in operation. The line which would connect the great system of the London and North Western Railway, by Tebay on the Lancaster and Carlisle Railway, with the Stockton and Darlington Railway, and thence with the West Hartlepool undertaking, would be opened during the course of the year.

In the light of this encouraging report it is not surprising that the resolutions passed at the meeting were full of praise for Sturge and his committee and for the Directors of the Company and, in particular, their Chairman:

> Moved by Nicholas Wood, Esquire, seconded by George William Rowley, Esquire, and carried by acclamation, – That the cordial thanks of the Proprietors be given to Mr. Ralph Ward Jackson for his unselfish and indefatigable exertions in the interests of the Company and its affairs and for his able and courteous conduct in the Chair this day.

Not a word of thanks for Coleman, but plenty of harsh criticism.

He must have anticipated this result of all his hard work and agitation, for he had already made preparations to carry on his campaign with even greater determination. By advertisement in the Press, above the name of his solicitors, Yarborough and Wilkinson, he invited the shareholders and bond-holders to a meeting in the London Tavern on the 1st of March, 1860. Wilkinson presided, and shorthand notes were made of the proceedings. Jackson was not there but he had some of his strongest supporters in attendance. The ostensible purpose of the meeting was to examine the Bill which had already been drafted and deposited in Parliament, in accordance with Sturge's recommendation. But very little was said about the Bill. The Chairman embarked on a long reiteration and amplification of Coleman's allegations, and indulged in a not very subtle smear campaign. What follows is a *précis* of what he and Coleman said:

(a) That the preference shareholders had preference even over the bondholders and Sturge's holding in the Company was £30,000 of preference shares – so he was safe, anyway.

(b) That Jackson, not so many years ago, was a humble attorney, "like myself", but now he was a great man, living at Greatham Hall, having apparently unlimited means, "so much so that he is the registered owner, in whole or in part, of ten collieries in the West Hartlepool district".

(c) That the directory of the West Hartlepool Company consisted of "Mr. R. W. Jackson; Mr. Charles Ward Jackson, who is his son, (his age believed to be between 25 to 27 years); Mr. Swainson, of Preston, his father-in-law and 80 years old; Mr. Robinson Watson, a woolen draper of Stockton; and Mr. Cuthbert Wigham, a gentleman who is very infirm and, moreover, blind". That two directors had seceded from the Board immediately before the 1859 Annual Meeting, and two others had previously resigned.

(d) That the balance of the Company's current account had been shown, in 1859, to be £21,775, but a year later it was said to be £578,109 – without any explanation.

(e) That although Sturge's report appeared to show that the Company was in a sound condition, he had privately said to Coleman – "Well, at all events, I am safe, and I think the bondholders are safe to a very considerable extent, possibly three-fourths, or something of that sort."

(f) That although Jackson had, in a letter, assured Coleman "that the Company do not possess, directly or indirectly, one inch of coal property in the kingdom; – they have no responsibility or connection with the working of any such property", it was now admitted in Sturge's report that the Company had interests in both collieries and steamboats.

(g) That the steamboats were being subsidised and had sought business by offering uneconomical freights on the regular services to Hamburg, Rotterdam and St. Petersburg. (The shippers at Rotterdam had been offered an initial 50% reduction below rates charged by other lines and, ultimately, a rate 2s. 6d. a ton below that charged by others.)

(h) That Sturge's report had disclosed that the authorised capital of the Company had been exceeded by £500,000.

Coleman made the curious statement – "I do not know whether you are acquainted with the subject of biology, or not. I am; and I believe that Mr. Jackson has a peculiarly strong power of this kind, a mesmeric power, so that every man that comes within the circle of his influence is biologised, and so brought to believe as he wishes, and that in something that really does not exist."*

The meeting ended without any resolution being proposed, and these words from the chairman – "I will merely say in conclusion, that if you are satisfied with the statement of accounts, or the non-statement of accounts, I am not satisfied until the accounts are furnished, and if any gentleman chooses to co-operate with me in any way, I shall be very glad of such co-operation. And, if not, I shall be very well content to do without it, and to seek redress in another way before a Committee of the House of Commons."

In fact, Coleman and Wilkinson had already Petitioned against the Capital Bill.

In March, 1860, Coleman published a 70 page pamphlet

---

*For further light on Coleman's belief in the power of mesmerism, see the Appendix – "Benjamin Coleman and Spiritualism".

entitled *An Address to the Proprietors and Debenture Holders of the West Hartlepool Harbour and Railway Company with Correspondence and Report of a Meeting held in the London Tavern on the 1st of March, 1860.* It was priced 1s. and contained, in addition to a rehash of his previous allegations, a copy of the correspondence which had passed between him and Sturge and a transcript of the shorthand notes of the meeting in the London Tavern. As a Postscript there was a copy of a letter, dated the 6th of March, 1860, written to him by one James Haldon, which said that, previous to the time of the last general meeting of the Company, Haldon had been asked by Admiral Cator what salary was paid by Coleman to Haldon's son, Samuel, who was employed in Coleman's counting-house. The information was not given, but the implication apparently intended was that Cator, or perhaps Jackson, wished to offer some inducement to young Haldon, in order to get information about Coleman and his activities.

The energetic and expensive steps taken by Coleman to try to frustrate the Company's Capital Bill of 1859/60, proved to be unnecessary, for the Board of Trade effected that result by their cool analysis of the Bill in their official report to the Select Committee appointed to examine it. It pointed out that the purpose of the Bill was to divide the Company's capital and debt between the railway and docks parts of the undertaking, and to increase the amount of the authorised capital and loan from £2,686,080 to £3,400,000, and said that the Preamble to the Bill gave the authorised capital as £2,014,560, and the loan debt as £671,520. It also pointed out that, before their Act of 1857, the Company's borrowing power had, by their Act of 1852, been limited to £521,520 and, although the Act of 1857 authorised the issue of additional shares to the amount of £450,000, it did not increase the borrowing limit. The Company had, however, assumed that their power under the Act of 1852 to borrow to the extent of one-third of their issue of stocks and shares, applied also to the additional share capital authorised by the Act of 1857. The Board of Trade also invited attention to the fact that no additional works were proposed by the Bill, and none had been authorised by the Act of 1857:

It may therefore be a matter of for inquiry whether the Company's powers for executing works have expired by lapse of time. It would therefore seem to require investigation, what has been the nature of the outlay which will exceed the £450,000 considered as sufficient in 1857, not only by the additional sum of £150,000, which the Company seems to have borrowed under a supposed authority from the Act of 1857, but also by further sums amounting to £713,920, for which liabilities have been, or are being, incurred by the Company, in anticipation of the powers sought for in this Bill.

With regard to the statement of Capital ... it may be observed that it does not appear how much of the capital of £526,400 and £450,000, authorised by the Acts of 1852 and 1857, has been paid up.

Section 28 appears to have for its object the legalising of all mortgages and bonds which the Company may have issued before the passing of the Bill, in excess of their present powers. Such excess may include not only the sum of £713,920, which is the difference between £3,400,000 and the present authorised capital and loan of £2,686,080 stated in the preamble, but also the sum of £150,000, if erroneously assumed to have been raiseable by loan, under the Act of 1857, and any sums which may have been raised by loan, instead of by calls, in respect of the amount not paid up on the preferential and ordinary consolidated shares and stock of the Company.

This adverse report was sufficient to make Jackson and his Board of Directors withdraw the Bill immediately before it was due to go before the Select Committee.

Coleman at once published another edition of his pamphlet, with an additional Postscript in which he claimed the credit for the withdrawal of the Bill, which, he said, implied that all his charges were true and that "the attempt on the part of Mr. Jackson, with the assistance of Mr. Thomas Sturge and Mr. Alfred Bell (*who was solicitor to both Jackson and Sturge*) to smuggle a Bill through Parliament intended to whitewash the wrongdoer, is an act of culpability and injustice". He alleged that, although Sturge had found an excess expenditure of £500,000, there was good reason to believe that the excess was over £1,000,000, and that the value of the Company's lands was no security for the illegal bonds, it being security only for the legal debentures; that the collieries and steamboats, "which the Company, for want of powers, cannot hold and work ... would be, as Mr. Jackson has already found them, ruinous to all concerned, and only useful to make a trumped up show of traffic, which has no real foundation of legitimate trading"; that Jackson had spent £70,000 per annum during the previous seven years to secure a nett revenue of little more than £100,000, and this had been concealed in the accounts; that if he had revealed it, it would have left him unable to pay any dividend on the stock and only half the interest on the preference shares and debentures; and that at least £150,000 of worthless debentures and "probably three times that amount", had been issued.

In June, 1860, the Company decided to call a special general meeting for the dual purpose of authorising the issue of new Debenture Stock and "to consider the course of conduct pursued by Mr. Benjamin Coleman, as affecting the Company, its business and officers, and to express the opinion of the meeting thereon, and to adopt such resolutions with reference thereto as the proprietors may deem proper".

Coleman had not confined his attack to the issue of circulars and pamphlets and Petitions against the Company's Bills. He had also availed himself of a weapon more directly effective to bring the Company to a standstill. On the 2nd of April, 1860, he had commenced Chancery proceedings for an injunction to prevent the directors from applying any monies of the Company to the purchase of steamers or other vessels, or of collieries, and to prohibit any loans to any company or person. And incidental to these proceedings he had asked for an order for the production of the Company's books and accounts.

He had no wish to be at the Special General Meeting to be held on the 28th of June, because it was to be at West Hartlepool, and previous experience had taught him that it would be packed with Jackson's supporters, so he wrote a letter to the local press telling the public that he would be prevented from attending the meeting because of the Chancery proceedings. This news would be more effective than anything he could have said at the meeting.

In May or June, 1860, he published a sixty page pamphlet containing a copy of correspondence which had passed between himself, Jackson and William Warne, the purpose of which was, apparently, to try to justify the continuance of his vendetta, in spite of the settlement of the dispute with Edwin Jackson.

On the 12th of July appeared another pamphlet from his vitriolic pen (40 pages, price 1s.), entitled *A Reply to the Proceedings of a meeting held at West Hartlepool on the 28th of June, 1860*. In it he sought to counter all that Jackson and his supporters had said at the meeting to praise and support Jackson and to blame and condemn Coleman. Much of it is a repetition of previous circulars and pamphlets with a long account of his version of his dispute with Edwin and of Ralph's part in it, but he also elaborated and added to some of his earlier charges. In particular he tried to show that Jackson's answers to those allegations had been designed to deceive, by the use of words which might be true in a strictly literal sense, but which really concealed the truth. For example, he said, Jackson had denied that he had issued a large *number* of debentures in excess of the authorised limit. But Coleman had never alleged a large *number* – he had alleged a large *amount* of such debentures and he instanced two of £34,000 each which he knew of, and repeated that the total was certainly not less than £150,000. Jackson had tried to confuse his listeners by drawing a distinction between bonds and debentures; by saying that he, personally, had not prepared any of the accounts of the Company; by, in one breath denying that there was a deficit of a million of money, but in the next breath admitting the expenditure of that sum by saying – "I have not got it, but I see it expended in the works before me."

Coleman said that the last report of the directors had shown an outlay on capital works of £2,543,140 and that they had unexhausted powers of raising a further £142,935, but it now appeared that the expenditure had been £3,300,000. In fact he believed that when the whole truth was known it would be found that the total outlay and liabilities had exceeded £3,600,000, but even on the admitted capital of £3,300,000, there must be a deficiency of £44,500 per annum, if interest were paid at the rates required, averaging $4\frac{1}{2}\%$ – "now, think of this enormous yearly deficiency going on for several years past and requiring fresh loans to meet it ... add the yearly loss on collieries and steamboats, and the whole mystery is solved of where a great part of the money has gone". He alleged that the great bulk of the consolidated share capital was in the hands of Jackson and his nominees, and had been pledged from time to time, and its place taken by debentures. In fact, he said, "the whole question is a debenture holders' question, and not a shareholders". And then he tried to destroy Jackson's main justification for his huge excess and illegal expenditure, which was that the trade of West Hartlepool harbour and docks had thereby been increased to an enormous size. He suggested that the trade returns were false, or manipulated in such a way as to give an untrue impression. He gave his version of how the timber trade had been secured from Hull and Grimsby and said that that trade would go back to those ports as soon as it ceased to be subsidised. He attempted to prick the bubble of the much boasted, and incredible, increase in the export trade of West Hartlepool, which has already been mentioned and which has gone into the histories of West Hartlepool and been repeated many times, with varying accuracy. It appears on page 47 of Martin's *Historical Notes* in the form of an extract from *Kitching's Tide Table* for 1861 (published at West Hartlepool):

Last year we had to record an astounding increase of the traffic at West Hartlepool. The declared value from Newcastle, Shields, Sunderland, Stockton and Middlesbrough, all put together, amounted to £1,384,646, while those from West Hartlepool alone amounted to £4,214,783, or upwards of three times as much as the whole of the five neighbouring ports put together.

Apparently the returns which had actually been made to the Board of Trade were even more "astounding", for they related only to the export trade and they were in respect of the year 1859. Here is how Coleman cast doubt upon them:

The most striking (of Jackson's "delusive misleadings") is the enormous increase in the amount of the Customs Foreign Exports from the port of West Hartlepool since the year 1853 which Mr. Jackson speaks of and paragraphs through the press on all occasions.

The directors' last annual report stated that the total gross revenue for 1854 was £129,732, (1853 is not mentioned). In 1859, the total gross revenue was £197,294, showing an increase in 5 years of £67,562; or about 52% only. The customs value of the Foreign exports for 1853 (1854 is not mentioned to prevent an exact comparison) was only £25,756. In 1859 it had attained the magnitude of £4,214,783; or more than 15,000% increase in 6 years on the value of goods exported, whilst the gross revenue has only increased 52% in five years. It is thus made clear that either Mr. Jackson grossly exaggerates the amount of the exports in 1859, or that he has carried on the trade at a ruinous loss to the Company.

Coleman's "Reply" went on to criticise the composition of the Board of Directors, then reduced as a result of "constant secessions" to the minimum number of five – Mr. Ralph Jackson, "whose untrustworthy character I have made sufficiently plain"; Mr. Jackson's son, Mr. W. Charles Ward Jackson, "an inexperienced youth"; Mr. Charles Swainson, Mr. Jackson's father-in-law, "who resides at Preston in Lancashire and is upwards of 80 years of age"; Mr. Robinson Watson, "a woolen draper, residing at Stockton who, very wisely, never opens his lips, and never takes publicly a part in the Company's affairs"; and, lastly, Mr. Cuthbert Wigham, "also upwards of 80 years of age, very infirm, and who is, moreover, blind". "Now, I venture to say that there is no parallel in any country for such a state of things as this".

He dealt with those directors who had resigned from the board, – Mr. Charles Barrett, "who has been from the start closely mixed up with Mr. Jackson's colliery transactions and who knows more about Mr. Jackson's peculiar dealing with the company's funds than any other man." Mr. Richard Fenwick, "who is upwards of 80 years of age and who has withdrawn every shilling of his capital out of the reach of his former 'highly respectable' colleague"; and Mr. John Winstanley of Preston, "the personal friend of Mr. Jackson's father-in-law, and who is, as I have been recently told, on the verge of 90".

Finally Coleman sought to destroy the dazzling prospect that Jackson was now trying to hold before his shareholders and the public of West Hartlepool of the huge "harbour of refuge". This would have involved the building of a long break-water over the Longscar Rocks to enclose, with an extension of the Hartlepool breakwater, an enormous area of the sea in which vessels could take refuge in bad weather. Coleman said that the Government had, in fact, made no decision about harbours of refuge and, in any case, the Royal Commission's recommendation was that £500,000 should be granted, but only after the Port and Harbour Commissioners had, themselves, raised and spent an equal sum.

The circular ended:

> It may be I, not Mr. Jackson, who will draw to light a band of conspirators from quarters little dreamt of, who are conspiring to impose upon your credulity, by attempting to uphold what, I am sure, will prove to be *one of the most stupendous impostures of modern times.*

In November, 1860, the West Hartlepool Harbour and Railway Company attempted to retrieve the desperate situation into which they were being driven by Coleman's attacks by promoting two Bills in the 1860/61 Session of Parliament.

One was a second attempt to get a Capital Act to increase their capital and to legalise their excess borrowing, and the other was a Traffic Bill to extend their running powers and to authorise the connection of the West Hartlepool harbour with the railway system of the London and North Western Railway Company; to empower the latter company to take over a quay and warehouse in the Swainson Dock and to acquire an interest in the West Hartlepool Company to the extent of a quarter of the share capital. The L.N.W.R. did, in fact, without Parliamentary authority, buy the warehouse and quay for £100,000.

Coleman again petitioned against these Bills and he launched a publicity campaign shortly before they came before Select Committees. His attack was directed principally against the Capital Bill. He issued an eleven page circular to the Share and Debenture holders on the 30th of March, 1861, the opening words of which were enough to daunt any Jackson supporter – "I was unable to be present at the last General Meeting of the Company by being in attendance until late the day previous in the Court of Chancery on the hearing of the Injunction Motion, in which the true state of the Company's accounts was for the first time made public. The result of the case was that the Vice-Chancellor, on my motion, put the company and the directors under an undertaking not to apply, until further order, any monies of the company in the purchase of any steamers or other vessels, or of any collieries, also not to advance to any company or person any money by way of loan, except the authorised advance to the Cleveland Railway". He warned of the two Bills shortly coming before Parliament and repeated much of what he had said in earlier circulars about the steamboats and collieries, the illegal borrowing, and then sought to chill the blood of those who might hold the debentures or bonds issued in excess of legal powers, by referring to the case of Pooley v. The Atheneum Company, "recently decided in Chancery", which, he said, proved that debenture bonds "issued beyond the number and amount allowed by the deed or Act of Parliament are

absolutely worthless even in the hands of a bona fide
holder who bought them in the market for value and in
ignorance of the fact". He urged the holders of legal shares
and bonds to see that the illegal debt "reaching, as it is now
ascertained, in the whole to nearly £2,000,000", should not, by
the Capital Bill, be brought in "to swamp the legal holders".

He said that the nine collieries, of which the Chairman had
for many years been the legal owner, and for which the
original purchase money had been paid in the Company's
bonds, had been, "year after year, running deeper and deeper
into the Company's debt for assistance bonds and unpaid dues,
the latter of which have formed the main excuse on which your
dividends have been based. In 1854 these nine collieries owed
you about £20,000, whilst today your colliery debt has
increased to upwards of £500,000. I have discovered too that
£117,000 has been surreptitiously laid out of the Company's
money in buying steamboats, and that, in one recent year, the
loss in one branch of these, was £10,000. Not a figure of all
this has been brought before you in any of the directors'
accounts, even with sufficient plainness to enable you to find
out that you had anything whatever to do with either
collieries or steamboats. The worst however remains to be
told."

The worst being that although the directors had, for several
years, declared that the ordinary paid-up share capital of the
Company was £815,855, in fact, because the market had never
valued the shares at anything like their par value, it had been
impossible to issue more than £288,000 of them. "Upon this
trifling basis, therefore, is erected a preference and loan capital
which is already admitted to be above £3,300,000. Even of this
£288,000, a considerable sum is not in bona fide hands, but
is only held by the chairman's son in trust for the company,
which is obliged, from time to time, to buy in from sellers
of shares to keep up the market ... Such a case as this is un-
parallelled in the worst history of directors' delinquencies."

Though it had nothing to do with the case, he threw in the
following smearing footnote:

Within ten days of the last general meeting, Mr. Ralph Ward Jackson, the chairman, having been convicted and fined £5, at the Sessions, for an assault upon another clergyman, the Rev. Mr. Tristram of Greatham, a policeman who was accused of perjury, and dismissed the Police Force, for giving evidence in favour of Mr. Jackson, was at once appointed to be one of your servants by Mr. Jackson. His attention to his new duties is, however, distracted by an indictment for perjury, which has been found against him at the last Durham Assizes, and is to be tried at the next Assizes.

He urged the illegal bond holders to demand that the Company should reimburse them immediately by disposing of the illegally held collieries and steamboats, and repaying them from the proceeds.

He said that the Company's expenditure now disclosed showed that if they paid $4\frac{1}{2}\%$ on the capital there would, after taking account of the alleged revenue of £112,846, be a deficiency of more than £50,000.

The actual deficiency, however, is much larger even than this, for you will observe in the last Report, that the largest item of the gross annual revenue is stated to be "Coal Traffic, £110,326. 19s. 2d." Now, fully three quarters of this alleged coal traffic is for carrying the coals from the collieries in question, of which I have before given you the history, they do not pay the dues but are yearly largely increasing their loss or nominal debt to the Company. The directors, however, to make up the revenue, not only put down the whole £110,326. 19s. 2d. as if it had been received ... but add the amount unpaid to the colliery debt; and, in addition, they add 5% interest to the colliery debt, amounting to £16,957. 8s. 10d., and then place that interest to disposable revenue, as if they had received it in cash, and available for dividend as profit. The same is done with the sum of £13,000, which is made an arbitrary addition to the land account, under the name of interest; and, although none of it is received, or likely to be, it is at once brought to disposable income, as if it had been received in cash, and is used to pay interest and dividends. The same is done by adding an arbitrary sum of £12,400 to an account for outlay on works as interest, and that sum, although it has no real existence, and is not and never can be received, is also made, in like manner, to do duty for dividend and interest.

He warned that by the Bills before Parliament it was proposed to reduce the minimum number of directors to three (Cuthbert Wigham having died) and this would effectively put the Company in the hands of the Chairman, his son and his father-in-law, or any two of them as a quorum.

He urged that another committee of investigation should be set up, but, this time, neither Mr. Sturge nor Mr. Nicholas Wood, should be members of it.

And, attached to his circular, he set out extracts from the Report of the Board of Trade to the Select Committee on the Capital Bill. This was largely a repetition of the points made on the Bill of the previous year. The new Bill proposed that power should be given to raise by borrowing an additional sum of £950,000, and the Report pointed out that this might lead to the Company's loan capital being in excess of one third of their share capital, which would be in breach of the Standing Orders which Parliament applied to railway bills. It also drew attention to the fact that the £950,000 was, under the Bill, to be applied towards the discharge of the debts and liabilities of the Company, "and for other purposes aforesaid". The Board did not like these vague words. They also referred to the proposal in the Bill that the excess bond and debenture debt was to be repaid "within 30 years", but there was no provision for the early commencement of the repayment "nor any positive security for its ever being effective". They thought that, if Parliament were prepared to legalise the excess borrowing, then consideration ought to be given to requiring the establishment of a sinking fund for the redemption of the debt out of revenue.

But they showed some sympathy for Jackson in his difficulties, and ended their Report thus:

My Lords have thought it right to call attention to the above points. How far the great and rapid increase of trade at

Hartlepool in recent years, which is adverted to in the Bill, and which is, no doubt, of great national importance, may be due to the facilities given by the works of improvement at West Hartlepool executed by this Company, is a matter not within the province of my Lords to inquire.

The Capital Bill came before the Select Committee in June, 1861, and Coleman's Counsel, Mr. Denison, did his best to persuade the Committee that the Bill was in a form that they ought not to allow to pass, and moreover that it could not be amended in accordance with the Standing Orders sufficiently to make it acceptable, and that therefore the Bill ought to be rejected and the Company left to promote a new Bill (which would have to wait for the next Session). If he had succeeded with that argument Coleman would have been able to bring the Company very quickly to a standstill, for their need for money was now desperate, and all potential investors and lenders would be likely to be on their guard as a result of the wide publicity which Coleman had given to his allegations.

Denison did not persuade the Committee to reject the Bill, but he did succeed in getting the next best thing, which was for it to be so restricted and amended as to make the Company's position virtually hopeless.

The Bill, as it was passed, was summarised by Coleman in another pamphlet of 51 pages (price, 2s. 6d.) which he published on the 27th of June, 1861, under the title – *Revelations in Parliament with the true state of the West Hartlepool Harbour and Railway Company's Capital Account and Shorthand Notes of the Decision of the Committee*. It was prefaced by a letter, dated the 12th of April, 1861, from his solicitors, which said "We learn from numerous sources that a rumour is being spread that Mr. Benjamin Coleman has left the country for America, and that he is not expected to return. We are able to say that he will be in London on or about the 14th proximo". For the reason for Coleman's visit to America, see the Appendix – "Benjamin Coleman and Spiritualism".

The pamphlet contained a reprint of Coleman's circular of

the 30th of March, 1861, and a long repetition of his previous allegations. He summarised the Select Committee's decisions thus:

Firstly – Not to legalise the sum of £507,205 spent on the collieries for which bonds had been issued.

Secondly – Not to allow the holding of the steamboats nor to legalise the sum of £120,000 spent on them by the Company for which bonds had been issued.

Thirdly – Not to allow the Company to contribute any further sums to the Cleveland Company. (*The Cleveland Company had been formed to make a railway from a point near Guisborough to Skinningrove and the West Hartlepool Harbour and Railway Company had been authorised to subscribe £60,000 of the share capital. Ralph Ward Jackson was its first chairman and among the directors had been his son, Robinson Watson, Charles Barrett and Cuthbert Wigham. The company had been conducted with Jacksonian irregularity and was, by 1861, in considerable difficulties. Nearly all the money spent by then had been advanced by the West Hartlepool Company. See Tomlinson's 'North Eastern Railway', p.597.*)

Fourthly – Not to allow the Board of Directors to be reduced to three.

Fifthly – General Meetings shall be held half-yearly instead of annually.

Sixthly – The Borrowing on loans of all kinds shall never exceed £700,000.

Seventhly – No borrowing power can be exercised until the whole capital is subscribed and half of it actually paid up.

The last two restrictions made the Act nearly useless to the Company, for their borrowing was already in excess of £700,000 and they could not raise money by issuing shares because no market now existed for their shares.

So Coleman had, effectively, won, but he was still engaged on his Chancery suit and the Act, as passed, specifically preserved his rights in that action, which was crawling along at the notorious snail's pace common to all Chancery

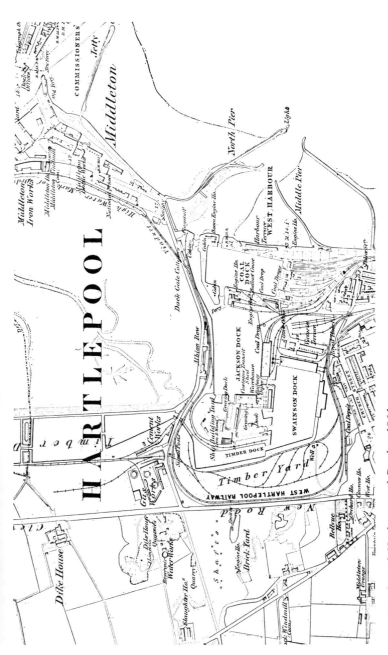

West Hartlepool Harbour and Docks, 1861.

The Town of West Hartlepool in 1861.

proceedings, and was affording endless opportunities for Coleman to subject Jackson to cross-examination and investigation, with all the attendant publicity calculated to damage the Company's reputation in the stock market.

The Traffic Bill, too, had failed to get the running powers needed to link the West Hartlepool system with the L. & N.W.R., and the latter had been refused power to purchase and hold the quay and warehouse in the West Hartlepool Docks or to take shares in the West Hartlepool Company. This may have been even more damaging than the restrictions in the Capital Bill.

Nevertheless Jackson tried to put on a brave face and, at the Annual Meeting of the West Hartlepool Company, held on the 22nd of August, 1861, a resolution of praise and thanks was bestowed on him and his co-directors for "bringing the Company to its present sound and prosperous condition" (see p. 38 of Martin's *Historical Notes*).

The fatal wound was inflicted by the Northern Assurance Company, who owned £38,000 of debenture stock in the Company, and had become alarmed about the value of their securities. They instituted proceedings in the Chancery Court in February, 1862, to obtain an order restraining the directors of the West Hartlepool Company from making any payment until the Court had taken action in the disposal of the assets among the creditors of the Company. The mess they were then in is described in Tomlinson's *North Eastern Railway* (pp. 599 *et seq.*). They owed more than £126,000 on overdue debentures. The Court appointed W. S. Leng, the Company's traffic manager, as Receiver and a committee of debenture holders appointed accountants, Quilter, Ball and Company, to investigate and report on the financial condition of the Company.

A new board of directors was appointed, consisting of five of the bond-holders, with Ralph Ward Jackson still as Chairman and Robinson Watson an additional member. On the 1st of March, 1862, this board had no option but to suspend payment of all further interest on debentures.

This did not prevent an individual bondholder from taking common law proceedings for payment of an overdue bond and, when judgment was given in his favour and the debt not paid, he obtained a writ of *fieri facias* to require the sheriff to seize sufficient of the engines, carriages and other property of the Company to satisfy the judgment. If one bondholder could do this, so could others, so the directors, with the sanction of the Chancery Court, immediately assigned all their property to W. S. Leng, the Court's Receiver, and thus blocked any similar moves.

Quilter, Ball and Company soon presented their report and it showed that nearly a million pounds had been expended by the Company in excess of their authorised share and loan capital; that, although the Company's accounts valued their surplus lands and the illegally acquired collieries and steamers at £983,228, their written-down value should have been only £677,735; that the debentures debt was £2,744,686, but if the Parliamentary limits had been observed, no more than £329,569 should have been borrowed – in other words, their excess borrowing totalled £2,415,117; and that only £14,628 remained in the revenue account to meet preference and debenture holders' interest totalling £168,224 – a nett deficiency for the year 1861–62 of £153,596.

On the 10th of April, 1862, Ralph Ward Jackson resigned from the Board of the West Hartlepool Harbour and Railway Company and, almost simultaneously, resigned from the Chair and Board of the Cleveland Railway Company. His reign as king of West Hartlepool was over, but his presence in and around the town would continue for some years more, and many of those whose fortunes he had founded would remain grateful to him and seek to preserve his reputation.

The steps which were taken by the new board of directors of what had been Jackson's Company, to try to restore the Company's viability are described in Tomlinson's *North Eastern Railway*. Briefly, at a great loss they disposed of the steamboats to Pile, Spence & Co., who agreed to continue the regular services to Hamburg and Rotterdam. They did so

under the name which Jackson had given to these services
– The West Hartlepool Steam Navigation. Soon Pile, Spence
would themselves go into liquidation, but the steamships
continued to operate under a company bearing the old
name, and the successor to that company still has its registered
office in Hartlepool.

In 1863 another Capital Bill was promoted, and this time
the remedies sought were more radical and drastic. All the
debenture stock was to be converted into 3% preference
stock. This would not only give the debenture holders
voting rights, but would, under the usual Parliamentary rule,
which Jackson has so flagrantly broken, enable the company
to borrow to the extent of one-third of the issued capital.
Although some of the old preference shareholders and
bondholders objected to their thus losing some of their
priority, this scheme was really their salvation, for it allowed
the Company to remain in existence, when otherwise it must
have been liquidated.

The Bill nearly failed to pass the House of Lords. Jackson's
manipulations and transgressions were severely criticised by
the Select Committee. However, the House eventually passed
it in order to prevent the hardship that would otherwise have
fallen on some of the innocent share and bond holders.
But it was a condition of their approval that the collieries
should be disposed of within five years and authority was
granted to borrow the necessary money to repurchase the
quay and warehouse which had been prematurely acquired by
the L. & N.W.R.

Tomlinson, who is the most respected authority on the
history of the North Eastern Railway, says, "Nobody in the
North of England doubted that the West Hartlepool Docks
and Railway would ultimately fall into the hands of the
North Eastern Company", and so they did, by agreement
reached between the West Hartlepool Company and the
N.E.R. Company on the 14th of November, 1864.
Strangely enough, in view of what he had suffered at the
hands of Coleman, but realistically enough, in view of his

very considerable holding in the West Hartlepool Company, the suggestion for the amalgamation came from Ralph Ward Jackson himself.

It was an agreement very favourable to the West Hartlepool proprietors, for it guaranteed to the former debenture and bond holders a preferential dividend of 4%, in perpetuity, and it guaranteed to the ordinary shareholders the same dividend, but, in their case, calculated on only £76. 19s. per £100 of their holdings.

Thus they emerged from their dire peril with the preservation of most of their capital and the guarantee by a huge undertaking to pay them a substantial rate of interest, which they would have had no chance of obtaining from the West Hartlepool Company.

The Bill to carry the agreement into effect was promoted in the 1864/65 Session and was strongly opposed by the port interests at Hull, who objected to the flat rates which the North Eastern Company were applying to the traffic which they carried from the North Eastern ports and which deprived Hull of the geographical advantage of nearness to West Yorkshire and Lancashire. But the Bill passed and, on the 1st of July, 1865, the West Hartlepool Harbour and Railway Company ceased to exist, having become part of the North Eastern Railway.

Evil Days

Ralph Ward Jackson continued to live at Greatham Hall and tried, embarrassingly, to offer his advice and services to the newly constituted board of the West Hartlepool Company during the brief period it remained in existence after his resignation. His letter accompanying his resignation shows how little the Coleman "Revelations", largely confirmed by Quilter, Ball and Company, had dented his self-confidence and self-esteem:

GREATHAM HALL
Thursday, 10th April, 1862.

My Dear Sir,

I very sincerely regret that I am prevented from being at the adjourned General Meeting of the West Hartlepool Harbour and Railway Company, at the London Tavern, on Friday next, the 11th instant. I have for several days been exclusively engaged under examination at Stockton-on-Tees, by order of the Court of Chancery in Mr. Benjamin Coleman's suit, and, out of the 100 days of the present year, I have been anxiously engaged, in travelling and from home on the Company's matters, for 92 days. I am suffering so much from fatigue of mind and body that I feel unable to undertake another journey to London today, in order to attend the meeting there to-morrow, which I fully intended to do.

Could I have been present I should have considered it my privilege to make some observations on the reports of the new Directors and Messrs. Quilter, Ball and Company, which reached me on Tuesday whilst I was under the Chancery examination referred to; but, as I cannot now be at the meeting, I address this letter to you for the purpose of reading it to the meeting, which I shall be much obliged by your doing at the earliest opportunity.

As to the Directors Report.

I am sorry to notice the harshness of such expressions in this report as that the directors "must express their sense of the unjustifiable and unwarrantable extent to which monies have been obtained and expended"; seeing that at least one-half of the total outlay of all kinds (and which is reported by Messrs. Quilter, Ball and Co. to be £3,733,393) consists of expenditure and engagements by former boards of Directors of the present and dissolved Companies previous to their amalgamation into the present company.

The Harbour, Sea, and Dock works at West Hartlepool are those which have absorbed the greater portion of the subsequent outlay and capital, and I fearlessly assert that nothing of the kind has been produced in this Kingdom equal to them at so low a cost, nor combining, for their extent, the like general adaptation, capabilities and economy of construction.

I have, indeed, stated to members of the new board of Directors, that I consider it would give general satisfaction if they would instruct independent Engineers of eminence to examine and report upon the present condition of these works; and I proposed that, if the Board felt any difficulty as to authorizing such examination and report for the Bondholders and Proprietors, I would gladly myself be at the expense of obtaining a report by any three Engineers whom the President of the Institution of Civil Engineers should select for the purpose, and that I would leave it to the proprietors and bondholders to refund the expense to me afterwards if they should think proper; but my suggestion and proposal have been discouraged.

Whilst, on the one hand, the new board of Directors have, by a general statement, alluded so strongly to the obtaining and expending of money for the concern, it is, on the other hand, worthy of remark that they have resolved to adopt the same measures to dispose of the Collieries as the late directors had recommended and the proprietors had agreed to at the Special General Meeting of the Company on 30th of August last; and I am glad to observe the opinion of the new directors that, "under assurances from several competent parties, this step may be carried into effect greatly to the Company's benefit"; and that it "will conduce to increase the mineral traffic on the railway and at the Port"; the new Directors adding, that they "are assured that the working condition of the collieries at the present time is most favourable for the introduction of private enterprise into their management".

I freely admit that considerable reductions can be made in the general working expenses of the concern, but, for the last three years, my time has unavoidably been occupied chiefly from home; and I, as one of the directors, have consequently been unable to give any material attention to the local management of the undertaking.

I am glad to perceive that the new directors attach importance to the Company maintaining communication by steam ships with Hamburg and Rotterdam – especially with the former; – that they believe that portion of the trade can be carried on with profit – and that they expect, at the next half-yearly meeting, to present a satisfactory report as to the reduction of working expenses, and to be enabled, "from their further insight into *the undoubted resources of the Company and the capabilities which exist for the development of its traffic*, to present a statement from which the proprietors may form some definite opinion as to the value of their undertaking;" – and, judiciously adding "they trust that neither the debenture holders nor the shareholders will be hastily led to part with their securities or property at an unnecessary sacrifice."

As to Messrs. Quilter, Ball, Jay and Company's
report –

It appears to me that those gentlemen, by not understanding the Company's various acts of Parliament, have been led into several miscalculations and deductions, and have exhibited some erroneous conclusions as to the Company's powers for share and loan capital, and that they have called that a deficiency which is no deficiency at all; because the amount is represented by at least an equal amount of large and valuable surplus properties and assets, amongst which are the steam ships, collieries, surplus land and houses, and interests in other companies.

Whilst the revenue, in 1853, was only about £72,000, it is found, for the year 1861, to be £216,661; but the deductions carried to the debit of it I feel are exceedingly severe and oppressive. Several large sums, which are usual and proper charges against capital, as for permanent outlay and not expected to occur again in future years, have been debited as working expenses or charges against this one year's income; as well as interest in respect of works not yet completed, and others unproductive; so that the balance of receipts and outlay on the revenue account for 1861 could not be made otherwise than unfavorable; but these deductions will not, I presume, again be made; and hence the future revenue, which the new directors themselves expect will continue to increase, may produce a much more satisfactory balance.

There is no doubt, that capital expended so rapidly in constructing Harbour and Dock works of such magnitude and importance as are now to be seen at West Hartlepool, cannot be expected to produce an adequate amount of revenue from such works alone, without more time for development than they have as yet had; but the Company are admitted to possess large and available properties and assets, amounting to nearly a million sterling beyond their undertaking and works, and such surplus properties and assets (some of which are unquestionably increasing in value), are obviously chargeable with all the Company's obligations, whether of principal, interest, or dividends, in addition to, and to the aid of, revenue arising from traffic on the works.

In regard to the capital account I deduce from Messrs. Quilter, Ball and Company's report, that the total amount of share and loan capital raised, and of outlay of every kind made to the end of last year, is £3,733,393, and that the surplus properties and assets, available to be realized without affecting the company's general works, amount – at a moderate computation and after allowing for considerable deductions – to £983,228. The cost, therefore, of the Harbour and Dock works, Warehouses, Railways, and Rolling Stock is reduced to £2,750,165, or £49,834 less than even the £2,800,000 assumed by Messrs. Quilter, Ball and Company to be the Parliamentary capital, though there ought to be also added to that amount the debts and engagements of the old dissolved companies (now comprising the present company), and which were also imposed upon the present company by the amalgamation act of 1852.

I hope I shall soon have the pleasure of welcoming you to West Hartlepool and of shewing you all that is to be seen in connection with the undertaking, over which I am happy to feel you now preside as the Chairman; and I shall be sincerely glad to render you and your colleagues every assistance which my health

will permit, towards the welfare and further development of the
concern, in which I have been most arduously engaged for
24 years of my life, – in which I must ever feel the deepest interest,
– and to the traffic and income of which I have had the greatest
satisfaction in being the means of contributing from £40,000 to
£50,000 a year, from sources over which individually I have
control, but without deriving from them one farthing of private
pecuniary advantage to myself.

> Believe me, my dear Sir,
> Yours faithfully,

HENRY R. SANDBACH, ESQ.,   RALPH WARD JACKSON.
    Chairman of the West Hartlepool
    Harbour and Railway Company.

But the new directors were not impressed by this bold
front and, far from feeling that they needed more of Jackson's
advice and help, were determined that he should no longer
exercise any influence on the Company or its officers. Worse
than that, they began to look at the books and accounts of
the three undertakings which had been amalgamated to form
their Company, and they were not satisfied that everything that
had been paid, or credited, to Jackson over the years from
1838 onwards, had been lawfully and properly paid or credited.
Neither were they satisfied with his son's account with the
Company.

After the letter of the 10th of April, 1862, had been read to
the General Meeting of the Company held on the 11th of
April, 1862, and it had become clear that the new Board
were not well-disposed towards Jackson, he and his son
became difficult to contact, notwithstanding that there were
several matters which needed their co-operation. For example,
shares had been vested in William Charles Ward Jackson
which were really intended to be held by him on trust for
the Company. And the colliery transactions were in a very
complicated state. Suddenly, the Ralph Ward Jackson who
had replied to all his correspondence so promptly and volumi-
nously, didn't reply at all, or only after months of delay;
documents which needed his, or his son's signature, were not

attended to; and, far from accepting that the Company might have any claims upon him, Jackson was urging the Directors to deal with his own claims against the Company for what he alleged were unsettled accounts for work he had done as Solicitor, Director and Chairman.

On the 18th of December, 1862, the solicitors who had acted for him in so many matters, but who were now the solicitors only of the Company, wrote to him:

> 49, Lincoln's Inn Fields,
> 18th December, 1862.
>
> Dear Sir,
> *West Hartlepool Harbour and Railway Company.*
> We are instructed to write to you upon the following subject:–
> The directors, in investigating your account with the Company, are considering an item entered as voted by the Dock Company and amounting to £8,000, paid to you on 27th August, 1851, and again placed to your credit in the Amalgamated Company's account to 30th June, 1854; also the year's interest charged in the accounts for the £8,000 after it had been paid to you, and the $4\frac{1}{2}$ years' charge at the rate of £1,200 a year from 30th June 1851 to 31st December 1855, besides the £800 per annum paid to you as Chairman of the Company; and also the repayments by the Hartlepool Pier and Port Commissioners of the Shipowners' Opposition expenses, which do not appear to have been repaid by you to the West Hartlepool Company.
>
> The directors hold a meeting here to-morrow, and will no doubt be at liberty to see you at half-past two o'clock, in case you should think it right to go into the question; and your doing so would be facilitated inasmuch as Mr. Baker and copies of the accounts are in London and will be here to-morrow.
>
> We remain, dear Sir, yours very truly,
>
> BELL, STEWARD, & LLOYD.
>
> Ralph Ward Jackson, Esq.,
> 11, Baker Street,
> Portman Square.

Jackson at first said he could not usefully discuss the matters referred to, as he hadn't all the books and papers with him, but he was willing "to refer the whole matter to arbitration".

However, after conferring with his new solicitor, Mr. Tyas, he wrote – "I have considered that I may as well, in company with him, call to see the directors in the hope that some arrangement can be made for going into an understanding and adjusting the accounts".

Tyas had a long interview with the Directors but they did not wish to see Jackson. The solicitor proposed that an accountant, appointed by Jackson, should be allowed to go into all the books and accounts. The Directors raised no objection but, without waiting for the result of that investigation, issued a writ against Jackson claiming £2,114. 12s., (presumably the sum paid by the Hartlepool Pier and Port Commissioners for reimbursement of Parliamentary costs).

On the 22nd of January, 1863, Tyas wrote a very long letter to the Directors, in which he tried to explain the matters which their solicitors had mentioned in their letter of the 18th of December. Summarised it said:

(a) That the two sums of £8,000 had never been paid to Jackson, but only credited to him in the books of the Hartlepool West Harbour and Dock Company and the Stockton and Hartlepool Railway Company.

(b) That these sums were to recompense Jackson for his work and expenses in acting for the two companies in many matters for which he had not been adequately remunerated.

(c) That, although there had been no formal vote at general meetings to approve these credits, the directors had approved them and the shareholders of the dock company knew about the £8,000 attributable to their company.

(d) That, although £10,000 of debentures in the Dock Company had been given to Jackson in settlement of his claim against that Company, a clerk had, mistakenly, credited £8,000 to him.

(e) That the two sums of £8,000 had been transferred to the accounts of the amalgamated company, the West Hartlepool Harbour and Railway Company, and had been passed and audited every year since the amalgamation.

(f) That if objection was made to the credits, then the whole question of Jackson's remuneration should be referred to arbitration.

(g) That the £800 a year was paid to Jackson only as Chairman of the Dock Company and the £1,200 a year was reasonable reimbursement of Jackson's expenses incurred on behalf of the Stockton and Hartlepool Railway Company and the amalgamated company.

(h) That the £2,114. 12s. had never been paid to Jackson by the Pier and Port Commissioners, but he had been given four mortgages, of £1,000 each, of the Pier and Port Commissioners' assets and these had been intended to be held in trust for the West Hartlepool Harbour and Railway Company and had, in fact, been assigned to the Company's Receiver.

After he had received the report prepared by Jackson's accountant, Tyas wrote again, asserting that, far from his owing the Company anything, "there is due to Mr. Jackson, in whatever way the case can be put against him, a considerable balance." They argued that the annual payments of £800 and £1,200 had not been director's fees (although the books described them as such), but were, in fact, reimbursement of out-of-pocket expenses, incurred while performing services other than those of a director, and that, if it were argued that a director could not, legally, act as solicitor to the respective companies, this was a mere technicality, and if the accounts were reopened, it would be found that Jackson was entitled to far more than he had received, or been credited with. They ended with the suggestion that there should be a mutual release of all claims by the Company against Jackson and by him against the Company. This was received without enthusiasm by the new Directors, who resolved, "that Mr. Tyas' proposal cannot be entertained".

After this the relationship between Jackson and the new

Directors deteriorated rapidly. They forbade their officers and employees to speak to him about the Company's business, or to give any information to him. They employed a blacksmith to fasten chains and locks on the doors of the rooms which Jackson had used in the Company's offices, so as to prevent him from removing books and papers. (On his solicitor's protesting about this the rooms were reopened, but Jackson was told that he must remove his personal papers without any delay.) He, for his part, became inaccessible and failed to answer letters from the Company's solicitors. When they became pressing he wrote:

At Exeter
3rd. October, 1863.

Dear Sir,

I have been travelling with friends in Cornwall, Devonshire, etc., and have not regularly received letters. Hence your two of the 19th and 28th September have not been earlier acknowledged.

I do not feel that I can, under all the circumstances, reply to them here and without mentioning the matters to Mr. Tyas, my solicitor, who I expect to see in a few days and, after that, to be at Greatham in about ten days.

I am sorry for the delay, but it cannot reasonably be complained of by the Directors; when, regardless of the impaired and delicate condition of my wife's health – the dying state of my mother – the dangerous illness and subsequent deaths of two other near and valued relatives, and disregarding all local and family ties and other considerations, it was, you know, wished and expressed to me that I should leave my home altogether and not approach within hundreds of miles of it and of West Hartlepool – a proposition to which it was, of course, no intention of mine to submit.

I do not forget – though I can overlook – the painful personalities to which I have been undeservedly subject and which I have hitherto borne in silence. I quite understand the relative positions of Shareholder and Director and the conduct and courtesies between each and between Gentlemen; and most assuredly can I declare that, on no one occasion, in no one instance, by action, word, or writing and to no Director or Officer, have I shown other than a kindly and honorable course of conduct.

I take this opportunity of suggesting – and it is my wish you should communicate this to each of the Directors – that I consider the time has arrived when some fair, honorable and general arrangement, with kindliness and consideration on all sides, should be brought about, and that the past and continuing anomalous, unpleasant and undesirable state of things with me on all matters should be thus terminated.

I remain, Dear Sir,
Yours faithfully,
RALPH WARD JACKSON.

John Tiplady Esq.,
Durham.

On Boxing Day, 1863, he wrote to the Company's Secretary, complaining about the instruction which had been given to the employees of the Company not to communicate with him, which, he said, was "being publicly and generally talked about and commented upon in the streets and town of West Hartlepool and elsewhere", and asked for a copy of the Directors' resolution. The Secretary replied that the Directors "entirely decline to furnish either the public or a shareholder with copies of their orders for the guidance of the Company's officers, or for the conduct of the Company's business." This brought a long letter from Jackson to the Directors, complaining of their attitude to him and emphasising that he only wanted to offer the assistance which he alone could give:

My long and intimate connection with the West Hartlepool undertaking in all its parts and in the district for twenty-five years, naturally entitles me – I say it not in egotism – to possess and impart, *if wished and fairly asked*, much more information on numerous important points than any of the present Directors can obviously be expected to have, or can actually obtain and usefully apply, during only the occasional and very short visits which you, as Directors, make to West Hartlepool, and more especially in regard to the works and further development of the concern, the policy and traffic of which, as established by myself and late colleagues, it is satisfactory to know you, as our successors, so completely adopt.

I only last week myself accompanied several gentlemen of the neighbourhood over the greater part of the West Hartlepool railway, to assist in the selection of a point for the establishment of large Iron Rolling Mills on the West Hartlepool system, and to furnish them with information as to sites and titles, etc., within my own knowledge; and I should have been glad if any of the Directors had been of the party.

He urged the new Directors to use the information and advice which he could offer on the improvement of the Hartlepool Bay and the implementation of the Harbour of Refuge scheme which he had prepared and which, he said, would not only add to the trade of the port, but would also protect the Company's works. He criticised the scheme which had been prepared by the Company's engineer for the improvement of the harbour. He went on at great length about his own and his son's claims against the Company and urged that one of the following courses should be adopted:

(a) He should be invited to discuss his claims with the whole of the shareholders at a general meeting, or

(b) He should discuss them with a deputation or committee which should consist of three or more proprietors, exclusively of each of the three, old, dissolved companies, and three or more proprietors of the present Company, or

(c) The whole matter should be referred to arbitration, "and I sincerely hope that whichever process is adopted, it will result in an early and inexpensive settlement, fair and honorable to all, and for ever put an end to the existing painful and undesirable state of things between parties who, really, have only one common interest and who should then, in every Christian spirit, let "bygones be bygones".

The reply was some three weeks in coming, and it was from the Secretary, Charles Baker:

WEST HARTLEPOOL HARBOUR AND RAILWAY COMPANY
Secretary's Office,
West Hartlepool – 4th February 1864.

Dear Sir,

I am directed by the Board to acknowledge the receipt of your letter of the 16th of January.

With reference to those parts of it which represent your anxiety to put yourself in intimate communication with the Directors and to assist them in the development of the Undertaking, and the value which you attach to the information you can communicate, the Board are of the opinion that the Company can derive no benefit from your assistance, or advice. But were it otherwise the present Directors could not disregard the painful facts connected with your management, nor the disastrous result which ensued from your unparalleled irregularities (to use no harsher term); and which eventually compelled the Company's bond creditors, to the enormous extent of two and a half millions of money, to submit to the grievous wrong of having their debts converted into shares.

The stain which you have brought on your character entirely precludes the present Board from accepting your services or assistance in any form and they are satisfied that, if it were for one moment believed that they were capable of accepting your co-operation and of permitting you to take any share in the management, their whole moral influence with the Shareholders and the monied interest would vanish and their future efforts to advance the prosperity of the Company would be paralized.

On this point they will gladly place themselves as you suggest, in the hands of the Shareholders who they are convinced will express their opinion in no unmistakable manner.

The present Directors have the satisfaction of knowing that hitherto at least the Company's position has not deteriorated under their management and they have as yet been at no loss and anticipate no difficulty in future in obtaining responsible advice in competent professional quarters upon any points of difficulty that may arise, whether engineering or otherwise.

I am to state that the directions given by the Board, that

the Company's officials should not discuss with you the Company's affairs but should refer you to the Board, were issued in no spirit of personal animosity; but for the simple purpose of protecting the Board from any unjust inferences, and the Company from any prejudice which might have followed your persevering attempts to identify yourself with the management of the Company's affairs in a manner never claimed by any other shareholder. The Board cannot be responsible for any misconstruction which you, or the public, may have put on this order.

As regards the Company's pecuniary claims upon you and as to any questions with your son, the former being the subject of pending proceedings in the Court of Chancery and the latter being in the hands of the solicitors of the parties, the Board decline any personal correspondence with you on these matters but leave them to be dealt with exclusively by their professional advisers.

The Board desire me, in conclusion, to state that they have taken no step against you but what appeared to them to be imperatively called for towards mitigating the serious pecuniary injury which the Company sustained at your hands, and that they are still actuated by the feelings which governed them at the close of 1862, when they uniformly declined, at their numerous meetings with the bond-holders, to become the instruments of initiating against you any measures of a different kind, which they were repeatedly urged to adopt.

I am &c

CHAS. A. BAKER.

Secretary.

Ralph Ward Jackson Esq.,
Greatham Hall.

It might have been expected that this chilling rebuff would have put an end to the correspondence, but Jackson had a remarkably thick skin, or, perhaps, a lofty indifference to the insults of his inferiors. Or, maybe, and more likely, he was writing for the record and future publicity. Whatever the reason, he quickly replied to Baker's letter, bypassing him and addressing himself directly to the Directors. He said he "regretted to observe the continuance – and that with aggravation – of the personal animus towards me" ... "repelled, with indignation, the strong epithets indulged in", denied that he had suggested that he should share in the management of the Company, emphasised that all he wished was to offer his unique knowledge and experience to the service of the Company, in which he and his family still held the largest number of shares, and complained that the Directors were unjustly blaming him alone for the misfortunes which had overtaken the Company:

> You isolate me for harsh personal attack – disregarding all former boards of Directors of the several Companies; all the yearly proceedings and confirmations of shareholders; the acknowledged legal validity of all the issued bonds and securities of the Company; the previous discussions and expositions to Parliament of the Company's accounts, finances and outlay; your own repeated statements and evidence to the proprietors, bond-holders and Parliament, of the soundness and value of the West Hartlepool Undertaking; its certainty, as you have announced, of its "discharging every obligation", its great capabilities; its undoubted and progressive revenue; its ample security; its "National Importance"; and the necessity for considerable additional outlay to provide for its increasing trade, which I and my late colleagues, you have testified, had so rapidly and largely secured and established to your hands.
>
> After all this – but still without denying that in the many difficult matters I and my colleagues had to encounter in this new and rapidly rising concern there may have occurred on our part errors of judgment, common to human frailty, and from which none of you, of course, can claim to be exempt; and, after my full and explanatory letter published in the *Times* of the 8th of September 1863, I do not consider it necessary to lengthen this letter by further remarks upon the second and third paragraphs of your last letter.

On the 27th of August, 1863, *The Times* had published a long leading article on the recommendations of a Select Committee which had been set up as a result of the Report on the West Hartlepool Company's Capital Bill of that year. The recommendations suggested some ways in which manipulations, such as those of the Company, might be prevented. The first sentence of the leading article was – "Lord Donoughmore and the other members of the Select Committee of the Lords on the West Hartlepool Bill have performed a public service by investigating the frauds which had been practised on the shareholders and creditors of the Company." In a later paragraph the writer said – "When existing companies undertake new works, there is no difficulty in preserving the proportion between the capital and the debts; but for several years it has been found impossible to fill the share list of any independent undertaking. Promoters are, therefore, forced to deal with contractors who accept shares in payment, and, in practice, the issue of paid-up shares in discharge of liabilities has been considered a sufficient justification for the exercise of the borrowing power." Jackson, in response to this leading article, wrote a letter to *The Times* which was published on the 8th of September, 1863. It contained more than 5,000 words! It is doubtful whether, nowadays, even a Prime Minister would be afforded so generous an amount of space to try to justify himself. As it is an outstanding example of the Jackson style, it is reproduced in the Appendix.

The new Directors decided to seek the approval of a general meeting of the Company to their attitude to Jackson and his repeated offers to assist the undertaking, and they prepared a report for the meeting which was to be held in London on the 26th of February, 1864. Jackson, learning this, entered into correspondence with one of the directors, Thomas Townend Dibb, of Leeds, in the belief that he was responsible for the report. Jackson threatened that if the report were to contain a personal and hostile attack upon himself, he would publish the correspondence that had taken place. Dibb said he must do as he pleased – "there is no wish on the part of the board to dissuade you from publishing the correspondence, if so advised."

On the 8th of February, 1864, Jackson did send a printed circular to the shareholders, setting out the correspondence and exonerating himself –

I am perfectly unconscious of the Company having sustained any pecuniary injury at my hands; and few will be hardy enough to deny that, if any other course had been adopted under the management of myself and former boards than what was pursued, West Hartlepool would never have risen to its present greatness, but on the contrary have been a failure, and with the Railways, Harbour, Docks and Warehouses, in a state of decay and ruin.

The Company cannot complain of my acts as in all they fully concurred and confirmed them; and if the Bond holders have suffered, it has arisen from an unparalleled combination of circumstances, and from such a pressure through rival ports, companies and parties, which no man or combination of men could, for the time, successfully resist.

The time, however, in which no one suffered more than myself, has passed over, yet I am still hostilely singled out by individual members of the present directory for continued personal attack, insult and unjust reproof, whilst my just claims against the Company remain unsatisfied, and my previous arduous and honest services, which established the present sound and progressive condition of the works and revenues, are cruelly ignored.

After endeavouring, most unfairly, to visit upon me the consequences of the present Board's own policy and act, namely, the compelling, – and as I believe, very unnecessarily – the Bond holders to convert their whole debts into shares, it pleases the Directors now to state – and that most unjustly – that the stain I had by that operation of their own, brought upon my character, precludes them from availing themselves – though nearly all are strangers to the district – of information and assistance which, as a shareholder, deeply interested with my family associations in the undertaking, and being connected with and resident in the neighbourhood, I am able and freely and honestly offer, whenever wished, to render to the Directors for the welfare of the Company.

To this I fearlessly reply that there is no such stain on my character, and that, although some errors of judgment, under the difficult process of establishing a new and rising Port, unparalleled in this Country for its success in the time, may, not unnaturally have been committed, by former Boards during their management, yet no human being will venture to assert that I have ever done anything for my own private advantage.

Neither have I, in my position as a Director, ever induced or accepted the offer of others, in their timidity, to part with their shares or property for my own benefit, on less advantageous terms, than, with a better knowledge, or more information, they otherwise might be entitled to.

On the 10th of April, 1862, I signified my intention to retire from official connection with the management of the West Hartlepool Harbour and Railway Company's affairs. I decided upon that step, solely from a feeling of honour that the new directors should have the most unrestricted and unbiassed means of investigating, in their own way, everything relating to the conduct and affairs of the Company from the earliest period, and I have faithfully observed that line of conduct which I prescribed for myself.

On my resignation I addressed a letter to the present Chairman, which was read to the Special General Meeting of the Company in London on the following day, the 11th of April, 1862, and a copy of which was transmitted to every proprietor. I concluded it thus ... [*see copy of letter ante p. 139*] ...

A personal and hostile course of conduct and proceedings having been adopted, in the name of the Board, towards me, it lately became painfully necessary, in justice to myself and acting under legal advice, that I should put myself in some cases, with respect to information and assistance, asked of me on behalf of the Board, in a position which I would most gladly have avoided, and which the following copies of recent letters will fully explain.

Notwithstanding the offensive personalities and adverse position thus taken, I was being pressed by Mr. Tiplady, the solicitor now acting for the company in the country, to assist the Directors by signing documents and searching for and letting them have papers and information to work upon; and observations were also being made that I was not properly attending to such businesses of the Company as I ought to do. I was not at home in September and October last, but receiving when at Exeter, letters from Mr. Tiplady to the above effect, I wrote him thus:–

(*Here follows the letter of the 3rd of October, 1863, reproduced ante p. 147, and other correspondence.*)

Whatever effect this 21 page circular had on the minds of the shareholders, it did not make them oppose the attitude of the Directors in refusing Jackson's offers of assistance and his claims on the Company.

On the 20th of May, 1865, the Company filed another Bill of Complaint in the Chancery Court. This recited alleged transactions by Jackson and his former co-directors in relation to land and collieries at Coxhoe and South Kelloe, which had, by a series of complicated mortgages and transfers, become vested in Jackson, subject to a mortgage to the Argus Insurance Company. As an additional security for this mortgage, it was alleged that Jackson had created, without any legal authority, 1600 shares of £12. 10s. each, in the Stockton and Hartlepool Railway Company. These had been converted into £26,666. 13s. 4d. of Consolidated Stock in the West Hartlepool Harbour and Railway Company, and had, eventually, become registered in Jackson's name. He had disposed of about half of this stock, but, after his resignation from the board, he still held more than £14,000 of it and, after paying off the balance due under the mortgage to the Argus Insurance Company, he claimed it as his own. The new Directors denied his right to it and asked the Court to order an account to be taken between the Company and Jackson and, in the meantime, to put an embargo on any transfer of the securities.

The actions commenced by the West Hartlepool Harbour and Railway Company were taken over by the North Eastern Railway Company after the amalgamation, and, as usual, they dragged on for years. In the end the Court absolved Jackson from any intent to defraud in respect of the £26,000 of Consolidated Stock and declared that he was entitled to it, but the N.E.R. were given judgment which allowed them to "surcharge" several of the items complained of and which totalled £21,000. In February, 1874, Jackson appealed against the decision but the appeal failed.

At the half-yearly general meeting of the North Eastern Railway Company, held on the 14th of February, 1873, the Chairman, the same George Leeman who, in 1855, had presented Jackson with his portrait in the Atheneum, made a speech in which he charged Jackson with having "deluded the shareholders of the West Hartlepool Harbour and Railway Company to the extent of £2,000,000 or so". Jackson commenced proceedings for defamation and the case was heard at the Durham Assizes, when the jury found in his favour, but awarded only nominal damages of 40s. Leeman appealed and the full Court of Exchequer heard the appeal on the 28th of April, 1874. They unanimously decided that Leeman's speech to the shareholders was a privileged communication and was one that he was not only authorised to make, but justified in making. Judgment was entered for Leeman and the Order of Mr. Justice Quain and the finding of the jury at Durham Assizes was overruled.

As Tomlinson says – "the long course of vexations litigation had ended in 'evil days'".

But there were many people in West Hartlepool who remained loyal to Ralph Ward Jackson. It had, by the end of his reign, become a town of about 16,000 people and it would continue to grow rapidly for many years afterwards. Good livings and, in a few cases, fortunes had been made and were being made, in shipowning, timber importing, and ship-building, as well as in numerous service industries and businesses which had sprung into existence because of Jackson's enterprise. It was of little interest to many of these people whether his methods had been strictly legal or ethical.

He remained a Pier and Port Commissioner and a Town Improvement Commissioner for some years after his resignation from the board of his Company (although Robert Martin says that after the Company's secretary, Charles Baker, had written to the town commissioners on the 29th of December, 1862, objecting to Jackson's acting as one of them, he refused to take part in their meetings). He was still a very influential man in the community and when the town, together with its neighbour, Hartlepool, was created a Parliamentary Borough in 1867, he was nominated as the "Liberal Conservative" candidate, in opposition to the "Liberal" candidate, Thomas

Richardson. The poll took place on the 17th of November, 1868, and Jackson was elected by a tiny majority of 3 votes, in a total poll of only 3097. Robert Martin says – "Jackson attributed his small majority to the fact that the North Eastern Railway, through its principal local officials, opposed his election". There was a petition against the election, but it was dismissed. However, Jackson held the seat only until the next election, in 1874, when he was defeated by Richardson by the large majority of 918 votes.

In the period following his resignation from the Board of the West Hartlepool Harbour and Railway Company he had had to endure sad changes in his family circumstances. In 1863 his revered mother, Susanna, who had lived at the Cottage at Greatham Hall for many years, died within a month of her 83rd birthday. Two years later his wife, also named Susanna, died at the comparatively early age of 59, and her body followed her mother-in-law's to the family burial plot in Eston Cemetery. His son, William Charles, had married in March 1863 and Ralph had had to face his trials and disappointments alone at Greatham Hall. After he had failed in his case against Leeman he left it and spent his last few years in London.

In the 1870s he made a few attempts to restore his fortunes by some mining and railway ventures in Derbyshire, schemes for supplying water to Cheltenham and for harbour improvements at Whitby, but these seem not to have been very successful, because, at the end of that decade, some of his friends felt impelled to assist him, and a fund of about £700 was raised (or promised) with which it was intended to buy him an annuity. But before that could be done, he died in London, on the 6th of August, 1880, aged 74.

The *South Durham and Cleveland Mercury* did not get the news of his death in time for their issue of the 7th of August, but, on the next Saturday, they printed a leader and a long obituary, which, because it contains interesting, though occasionally slightly inaccurate, biographical information, and gives an impression of the general attitude of West Hartlepool people towards him in 1880, is reproduced in the Appendix without any attempt at correction of one or two obvious errors.

Separate from the obituary was this rather pathetic little notice of the funeral:

THE FUNERAL

The remains of Mr. Jackson were interred on Monday morning, in Kensal Green Cemetery, London, the utmost privacy being observed. Most of the tradesmen in West Hartlepool paid a fitting token of respect to the memory of the deceased gentleman, by closing their shops at the hour at which the funeral was announced to take place. Flags were hoisted half-mast high, and the bells of Christ Church were tolled.

On the evening of the day of the funeral Parson Rudd preached at a memorial service in Stranton Church and the *Mercury* gave a short report of the sermon, which included this:

He fought his way manfully, but not for himself alone. He provided bread indirectly for thousands, and others had followed him who now reaped the result of his labours, and in the midst of all he endured much weariness and painfulness. His task was at last finished, and we might say, in language sometimes too thoughtlessly uttered over the grave of departed friends, "We give thee hearty thanks for that it hath pleased thee to deliver this our brother out of the miseries of this sinful world." We all regret that he has not this day been gathered to the grave of his fathers, when doubtless, from a sense of loyalty to his memory and a sense of duty we should have attended the last mournful office performed over his ashes, because we all know that it is to his energy and industry the development of the port is entirely due. He was also ever ready to dispense of his charity, and at all times anxious, to a fault say some, to find work for the toiling masses.

During the week following his death a meeting was held in the Atheneum at which there was a discussion about what should be done with the money, or the promises of money, which had been given to buy an annuity for him. Various suggestions were made – a statue, a stained glass window or a park – but in the end this was the resolution which was passed:

> The lamented death of Mr. Ralph Ward-Jackson having frustrated the design of this committee, resolved that the secretaries communicate his death to the subscribers, and inquire whether, having regard to the invaluable services rendered by the deceased in founding and nursing this port and town of West Hartlepool – services extending over many long and laborious years, and characterised by continuous and unselfish devotion, they would consent to allow the whole or a portion of their promised subscriptions to be applied by this committee towards perpetuating the memory of the deceased in the town of his creation.

The subscribers must have agreed, and others must have added to the fund for, on the 30th of December, 1881, the trustees paid £1,700 to William Alexander Wooler for the purchase of the site of the small but beautiful park which lies on the West side of the town. It was vested in the Town Improvement Commissioners, who laid out the park which, by the trusts in the deed of conveyance, was to be known as "The Ward Jackson Memorial Park". It is still known by most of that title, though the word "memorial" has slipped out of use, and it is still the most popular park in the town.

And in other ways his friends remembered him and perpetuated his name. There is, or was, a Ward Jackson School, a Ward Jackson Hotel, a Jackson Arms public house, and, in 1895, Colonel John William Cameron, the proprietor of the town's large brewery, Commanding Officer of the 4th Durham Artillery Volunteers, an Alderman and former Mayor of what had then become the Borough of West Hartlepool, decided that the 50th anniversary of the opening of Jackson's harbour should be marked by the erection of a statue, which he would provide, and which would stand at the head of Church Street. It was cast in bronze, cost about £2,000, and was unveiled on the 12th June, 1897, by the Marquis of Londonderry.

Inquest

There can be no reasonable doubt that the man who was directly responsible for Jackson's downfall as the chairman of the West Hartlepool Harbour and Railway Company was Benjamin Coleman, and there can be little dispute that he would never have known anything about Ralph Ward Jackson if he had not become involved with Ralph's brother, Edwin, in faraway Liverpool. But the question that has intrigued everyone who has been interested in the history of West Hartlepool is who was behind Coleman in the long, difficult and expensive campagin which he waged to secure the downfall of this man who had done no more to his injury than to appear as a witness against him in the libel proceedings which he had instituted against Edwin, and to act as Edwin's legal adviser and supporter in the prosecutions and the arbitration which followed them?

Perhaps one ought first to ask whether it is necessary to assume that anyone was behind Coleman. If there were not, one must be prepared to believe that this man:

who had repeatedly demonstrated his desire for money,

who had failed in business more than once,

who had been paid every penny he could claim, either in law or in honour, to have been due to him from Edwin, and had, moreover, been awarded and paid £400 damages and his costs,

should be so imbued with the desire for revenge that he would:

voluntarily, and when within sight of being paid off by Ralph, at a cost of £70 acquire £100 of Consolidated Stock in the West Hartlepool undertaking,

embark on a campaign involving the printing and publication of seven pamphlets or circulars, some of them very lengthy and some running into several editions,

institute and prosecute Chancery suits which went on for years,

make visits to many parts of the North of England from his home in London,

lodge petitions against several Bills in Parliament and, subsequently, engage counsel to argue against them, without hope of obtaining his costs from the promoters,

make appearances before general meetings of the Company

at which he would be given very hostile receptions solely for the purpose of bringing the undertaking of which he had become a shareholder to ruin. It is not credible, and, certainly, Ralph Ward Jackson did not believe it. He challenged Coleman to name those who were supporting him. During the Chancery proceedings Jackson's counsel closely examined Coleman on the subject, but without success. Jackson said that Coleman's own friend and arbitrator, William Warne, had hinted that Coleman's imputations had possibly been suggested to him by malevolent parties and that he might have been "induced to take a position from which he could not recede": In his circular to the shareholders dated the 18th of January, 1859, Jackson said:

> Being desirous of ascertaining who might be behind the scenes, I offered to face Mr. Coleman before the Chairman and the Secretary of the London Stock Exchange, and to place in the hands of that Chairman £200, to be distributed, of his own discretion, among any of the charitable institutions for the poor in London or elsewhere, on Mr. Coleman's disclosing the names and addresses of all or any of the persons from whom he states he received his information or with whom he might be co-operating; but Mr. Coleman would not accept my offers.

Who gave the Game Away?

It would be common knowledge to those who were engaged in the shipping and commerce of West Hartlepool that Ralph Ward Jackson was the registered owner, or part owner, of the vessels that were providing the regular services between the port and Hamburg, Rotterdam and St. Petersburg. The port register provided the proof. Not so readily accessible to public knowledge was the fact that nine or ten collieries which sent all their coal for export to the West Hartlepool coal drops were either in the ownership of, or in some sort of arrangement with Jackson, but it cannot have escaped the attention of people who carried on the business of the port that these collieries were the backbone of the coal traffic, and it must have seemed curious to those who kept the books of the collieries that, in many instances, and over several years, the port dues were not being paid.

This knowledge may have had little significance to the man-in-the-street, but to anyone familiar with the powers under which railway and port companies usually operated, and particularly to those who might view with envy and concern the, apparently, stupendous increase in the trade of the Port of West Hartlepool, and the transfer to it of traffic from rival or neighbouring ports, it was likely to give rise to questions and suspicions.

So, when Coleman decided to see what he could get out of Ralph and his family by publishing his pamphlet on the dispute and proceedings between himself and Edwin, he was soon in receipt of some information from ill-wishers towards Ralph which made a man of his experience and knowledge of company affairs suspect that there was a promising field to be investigated in West Hartlepool.

The ill-wishers were numerous, but which of them took the trouble to write to Coleman to encourage him to pursue Ralph is a matter of pure conjecture. One could line up the categories of suspects thus:

(i) Many of the people in the ancient Borough of Hartlepool who, rightly or wrongly, felt that Jackson had deprived their port and town of much of the prosperity which otherwise might have belonged to them and which had been promised by Christopher Tennant when the Act was passed to bring the Clarence Railway coal to old Hartlepool. Although not an inhabitant, Rowland Burdon junior, the man mainly interested in the Hartlepool Dock and Railway Company after his father's death, was one of Jackson's persistent and life-long opponents.

(ii) The Rev. John Hart Burges and his friends and supporters in the Christ Church affair.

(iii) The port and shipping interests at Hull. Jackson had taken from Hull and Grimsby a considerable amount of their timber trade and Hull felt jealous of the coal export traffic at Hartlepool and West Hartlepool. They strongly opposed the Bill for the amalgamation of the West Hartlepool Harbour and Railway Company with the North Eastern Railway Company. Tomlinson says – "The progress of the northern ports was almost regarded as an affront to Hull. 'You have only to unfurl a flag with "Hartlepool" upon it', said Sir Edmund Beckett, in addressing a Select Committee in 1880. 'and Hull takes fire immediately'."

(iv) The port, railway and shipping interests of the River Tees. Jackson regarded Stockton and Middlesbrough as the principal rivals to West Hartlepool and he had had bitter experience of the lengths to which the Tees Conservancy Commissioners would go to try to frustrate his ambition to take a share of the iron ore traffic from the Cleveland area. The "Battle of the Tees" is recorded in some detail in Tomlinson's *North Eastern Railway* and is also reproduced in Martin's *Historical Notes*.

(v) The Stockton and Darlington Railway Company, four of whose representatives were also Tees Conservancy Commissioners. Joseph Pease, who had been one of the founders of the Company, was also one of the founders of Middlesbrough. He became a leading opponent of Jackson and his West Hartlepool Harbour and Railway. Jackson reciprocated, and more than one

The original offices of the Hartlepool West Harbour and Dock Company in Victoria Terrace (photographed in 1972).

West Hartlepool Harbour and Railway Company's Offices in Mainsforth Terrace, photographed in December 1972, shortly before their demolition. (The archway was the entrance to the old passenger railway station.)

Parliamentary Select Committee hearing was enlivened by a spirited contest between these two men.

(vi) The North Eastern Railway Company, whose tentacles were, by 1859, about to draw into its control all the railway systems in the North East of England and for which the independence of the West Hartlepool Harbour and Railway Company, with its interest in linking up with the London and North Western Railway Company, was a blot on an otherwise beautiful landscape of monopoly.

Beyond these there must have been many individuals who had come into conflict with a man like Ralph Ward Jackson, and who would have liked to see him brought down.

Coleman's own account of how he was attracted to the hunt is contained in his pamphlet of the 12th of July, 1860, addressed to the Share and Debenture Holders of the West Hartlepool Harbour and Railway Company, in which he gives his potted version of his dispute with Edwin and the account of his publication of the "Libel" pamphlet and his visits to the North (*see ante p. 104*).

He said:

I then heard of various things connected with his (*i.e. Ralph's*) policy and conduct in the management of your affairs, which assured me there was ample room for enquiry into what, as I afterwards found, Mr. George Bidder, the eminent engineer, had described before a Committee of the House of Commons as something "very rotten in the state of Denmark", and I determined to investigate it for myself. I accordingly sought an interview with two gentlemen, who had been Mr. Jackson's colleagues, and had seceded from the direction of your board. Here, again, I heard from one of them of an act of surprising baseness and perfidy on the part of Mr. Jackson of which I shall presently speak. It was no mere imaginary matter. The evidence in writing was laid before me, and it was really shocking. To enable me to investigate the accounts I had ordered Mr. Bazett Jones, share broker of Preston, to buy me £200 or £300 of West Hartlepool Stock and I returned to London on the 3rd of October, 1858.

So it would seem that Coleman had learned enough in Lancashire to make him decide it would be worth-while to buy some stock in the West Hartlepool Company, but it could well be that so cunning and devious a character as he would have designedly put his order through the Preston stockbroker for the purpose of frightening Jackson, for he says:

> I have no doubt he immediately informed his patron of my desire to become a shareholder in the West Hartlepool Company, for, on the 8th of the same month, Mr. Jackson wrote a con-ciliatory letter to my friend, Mr. Warne ... and therein offered his services in bringing about a final settlement of the matter between me and his brother.

What Coleman may have learned, apart from any personal grievances or disputes, would probably be no more than the suspicion, if not knowledge, of these former directors that Jackson had acquired the collieries and steamboats, and that borrowing had been taking place on a scale far greater than that disclosed in the Company's accounts. Originally Cole-man seems to have thought that he was "on a better thing" than ultimately turned out to be the case. He suspected that Jackson had acquired the collieries and steamboats as a private speculation and had been subsidising them out of the Company's funds for his personal gain. But at the end he was alleging something quite different – that the collieries and steamboats, although acquired in Jackson's name, were really the property of the Company, and that from the beginning they had been worked at a ruinous loss, which had had to be covered up by failure to collect the dues owed by the collieries and by an ever-increasing borrowing from bond and debenture holders.

Who was behind the Scene?

As to who may have backed Coleman financially in his campaign, we are confined to a smaller but more obscure field of speculation. If there were backers, Coleman would not be likely to name them, but he did devote a good deal of space in one of his pamphlets to saying who they were not.

Jackson had his suspicions that they were "parties at Stockton, Middlesbrough etc. (in which enemies of West Hartlepool are known to exist)", but Coleman dismissed this suggestion in his own devious way. Referring to Jackson's speech at the general meeting of the Company held on the 28th of June, 1860, he alleges Jackson said – "But Mr. Coleman is not alone in this matter; there is a conspiracy behind; a conspiracy is a very difficult thing to make out, but that conspiracy is drawing to light. Mr. Coleman himself has been examined upon oath. His statements are in writing and whether they will be published will depend upon himself. But they are there. I have not the documents here, and will not mention names." Coleman continues:

> Now Mr. Jackson means you to understand that having been under examination in the Court of Chancery, I had confessed that I am acting in concert with parties in his neighbourhood, and that I had acknowledged to certain names by which the conspirators "are drawing to light".
>
> I have to assure you that there is not the slightest foundation for this most daring and impudent falsehood. It is true that Mr. Jackson obtained an entire day to examine me, as he was entitled to do, on my affidavit, when his counsel found my answers so unpalatable and damaging to Mr. Jackson that he abandoned his task in an hour.
>
> I was asked a great many irrelevant questions, which Mr. Hobhouse, my counsel, advised me I need not answer; but as I had nothing to conceal I did not avail myself of the privilege; and, as Mr. Jackson says, my answers "are there in writing", that is, they are recorded in the Chancery proceedings; and he is bold in his falsehood in the confidence that I cannot reply at once to him without prejudicing my position with the Vice-Chancellor, whose opinion has been already elicited, upon the complaint of Mr. Jackson as to my last pamphlet, on the imprudence of publishing anything on the subject pending the suit.

But Mr. Jackson is mistaken, for as he has now given me the opportunity, and has made it my duty to put forward the truth, I am determined not to allow his "lies" to pass current, even for a day. You shall therefore know the nature of Mr. Jackson's interrogatories and my replies on the occasion of my examination.

The whole object of the examination was, of course, to know with whom I was acquainted; from whom I had obtained information upon which my charges were founded; and whether certain parties were not pledged to pay the costs of the suit in Chancery. The names of several gentlemen were put to me, and I was asked whether they had not given or promised to give me pecuniary aid in support of these proceedings, and in each I answered truthfully – "No!"

It was then put to me, whether I had ever given information to the Stockton and Darlington Board or Company, and whether I had ever received any assistance in money from them, or promises of any kind. To which I answered – "No, never."

For some reason, I was not asked as to my knowledge of or connection with any one residing at either Stockton or Middlesboro', and the omission was remarkable, inasmuch as Mr. Jackson and his press have repeatedly insinuated that certain parties in those towns have been in very active communication with me, and that I had derived much information and support from that quarter, particularly from one gentleman who holds a high official position, and who in the discharge of his duties, is in frequent collision, as I know from published statements, with Mr. Jackson, and who is also the legal adviser of a lady holding a very large interest, one of the largest I believe in the West Hartlepool Company; and this lady, by the way, who was formerly on intimate terms with Mr. Jackson and his family, presented a petition against Mr. Jackson's money bill containing some grave charges of misleading. The gentleman I here allude to is Mr. Joseph Dodds, of Stockton, the law clerk to the Tees Conservancy Commissioners. I mention his name thus publicly and without his knowledge or sanction, for the purpose of doing him an act of justice, which I was precluded from doing in my examination by Mr. Jackson's studied avoidance of it, and because I know that Mr. Jackson has charged him with supporting me, and has thus attempted to lessen Mr. Dodds' influence with his respectable clients. I am acquainted with Mr. Dodds, it is true. I called on him two years ago as a stranger, and asked him to take charge of my case professionally. He declined to do so, because of the peculiar position in which he was placed, *and from that time to this I have never received information or support from him of any kind whatever.* I know, however, from printed and other documents, that Mr. Dodds has the lowest possible estimate of Mr. Ralph Ward Jackson's honour and general truthfulness; – and I saw in a recently published correspondence that he stigmatised a statement made by Mr. Jackson as being "a falsehood from beginning to end". Indeed, even Mr. Thomas Wilde Powell, who supported Mr. Jackson at the late meeting, also admitted to me that Mr. Jackson was a person who was notorious for his total disregard of the truth.

In returning from this digression to the subject of my examination, which Mr. Jackson has so imprudently challenged me to make public, I was further asked by his counsel, Mr. Robinson, if I knew Mr. ——— (a gentleman who had been a director in the West Hartlepool Company, and in most intimate social relations with Mr. Jackson and his family) and I replied, "Yes, very well." "When did you see him last?" – "About three weeks ago." "When, before that?" – "About a month or two previously." "Did he give you any information?" – "I don't think he did on that occasion; but I gave him a good deal." "Did you speak of West Hartlepool affairs?" – "Yes, we seldom talked about anything else." – "When did you make his acquaintance?" – "About 18 months ago." "What did he say to you then?" – "I think you had better not press me on that point." "I shall ask you any questions I please; you may refuse to answer if you like. Now, sir, what did he say?" – "He told me that Mr. Ralph Jackson was a man he would not believe on his oath," and that "he had been concerned in a most disgraceful transaction, and he was a person for whom he had the most perfect contempt."

Mr. Jackson here whispered to the counsel, and I was asked "When you speak of a disgraceful transaction, you do not mean that Mr.—— spoke of a money transaction. It was not, I believe a business matter. The question, in fact, was a matter more particularly affecting Mr. Jackson's son, was it not?" – "It was not a business transaction, certainly, and Mr. Charles Ward Jackson was mixed up in the disgrace, but Mr. —— applied those remarks specially to the father, and not to the son."

After this, some very trifling questions were put, and the proceedings terminated, as I have said, in little more than an hour.

If we accept Coleman's statement at its face value, and no more than its face value, we are left with this:

He denies that he acted "in concert with parties in the neighbourhood" – by "the neighbourhood" he here, presumably, means – Hartlepool, West Hartlepool, Stockton and Middlesbrough.

He specifically denies that he had received "any assistance in money", or "promises of any kind", from the Stockton and Darlington Railway Company or its Board.

He denies that from the time when he asked Joseph Dodds, the law clerk of the Tees Conservancy Commissioners, to act for him, he had received any information or support from him.

That narrows the field of suspects, but it does not necessarily exclude individuals who might be on the Board of the Stockton and Darlington Railway Company, and, to a suspicious mind, it does not necessarily exclude the Tees Conservancy Commissioners.

To make a realistic guess one must give great weight to motive and to the scale of expenditure which was involved in the pursuit of Jackson.

The West Hartlepool Harbour and Railway was, by the end of 1859, a large undertaking and had rail connection with a wide area. It was, because of its immediate access to the sea and an abundance of level land available for quays, railways, and storage grounds, able to handle shipping, to load and discharge cargoes, particularly of coal and timber, more expeditiously and economically than any other port on the north-east coast. Therefore, the destruction, or liquidation, of the West Hartlepool Harbour and Railway Company would not necessarily, or even probably, eliminate the West Hartlepool Harbour and Docks from the field of competitors for the shipping trade of the north-east coast, but, on the contrary might facilitate their acquisition by some more powerful company. It would not restore the coal trade to the River Tees, or the timber trade to Hull. There were, then, only two likely sources from which Coleman might have sought and received a promise of financial support.

One was the Stockton and Darlington Railway Company. Coleman had categorically cleared that company and its board, but that did not necessarily mean that he had eliminated from suspicion individuals with seats on the board or with large interests in the company. Such individuals would include members of the Pease family, who had been closely involved with most railway ventures in the North-East. Joseph Pease was "the most representative figure in the history of the Stockton and Darlington Railway" (Tomlinson – *The North Eastern Railway*), and his eldest son, Joseph Whitwell Pease, would be made a director of the N.E.R. on the amalgamation of the Stockton and Darlington with that company in 1863. The Stockton and Darlington board had their eyes on the West Hartlepool undertaking in 1859 and, at the same time, negotiations were pending for a working arrangement with the N.E.R.

The other was the North Eastern Railway itself. In 1857 the formal amalgamation of the Hartlepool Dock and Railway Company (the old Hartlepool Company) with the N.E.R. had taken place, the swallowing of the Stockton and Darlington Railway by the N.E.R. was in view, and the West Hartlepool Company would be the only fly in the ointment after that. And they were engaged in irritating, indeed frightening, negotiations with the London and North Western Railway. If that company gained an important foothold on the north-east coast they would constitute a real threat to the envisaged monopoly of the N.E.R. George Leeman, the deputy chairman of the N.E.R., had been a close intimate of Jackson since Jackson's earliest days in West Hartlepool. But he was his rival by 1859. Soon he would be involved in the vexatious litigation with Jackson that was to end in Jackson's "evil days".

There would be great gain to the N.E.R if the West Hartlepool Company could be brought to liquidation, for then it could be acquired for far less than would have had to be paid if Jackson had been able to maintain the appearance of a flourishing and growing concern, making large profits and extending its operations into Cleveland and westwards.

The choice of backer, if there were one, seems then to lie between the Stockton and Darlington Railway Company, acting through a representative, and the North Eastern Railway Company. Perhaps both were involved. But, it must be emphasised, this is mere conjecture.

Verdict?

To attempt to give a verdict in this inquest, when so much has been conjecture and hearsay, would be unjustified and presumptuous. But it would also be unfair to Jackson and his memory simply to end the story where it is now, leaving the reader to form his own opinion on what has been related in this book, when so much of it is coloured by the spite and innuendo of Coleman.

As to Jackson's honesty, these facts seem relevant:

(i) Sturge's Committee of Assistance, whilst confirming the illegal acquisition of steamboats and collieries, and some of the excessive borrowing, had imputed no motive of personal gain or fraud to Jackson. On the contrary, they had tended to justify these irregularities as being in the interests of the company.

(ii) The Chairman of the Select Committee of the House of Commons on the 1861 Capital Bill, had said:

> There is just this I would wish to say. That with regard to Mr. Jackson personally, the Committee are of opinion – of course they cannot shut their eyes to the fact that he has acted very hastily and very rashly – but, at the same time, they do not attach to him, in any shape, any criminality, or that he did anything for his own personal benefit; he acted very rashly, and perhaps has compromised others by raising these legal questions; but, in justice to his character, I think it right that I should state that.

Mr. Denison, (Coleman's Counsel), chimed in:

> That is what I should have said myself if I had been going to make a speech. I think he has been led by his zeal for the company to do many things irregularly. Personally, I have nothing to say to it – not a word – still that does not quite get us out of our difficulty.

(Coleman did not agree with these generous sentiments, for, in quoting them, he draws attention to the provisions of the Fraudulent Trustees Act, 1853, which he thought Jackson had infringed.)

(iii) The Select Committee of the House of Lords on the 1863 Capital Bill, presided over by Lord Donoughmore, had not been so convinced of Jackson's innocence. In answer to a letter from Jackson asking to be heard by the committee, Lord Donoughmore had summarised the charges against Jackson and his co-directors as follows:

1. Borrowing money in excess of Parliamentary powers.
2. Expenditure of the Company's funds for purposes other than those authorized by the Acts of Parliament, particularly in the purchase and working of collieries and steam vessels.
3. Neglect to collect dues from the owners of certain collieries, by which the Company suffered considerable loss.
4. Illegal subscription to the funds of the Cleveland Railway Company beyond the limits fixed in the Act of Parliament.
5. Mortgaging the Company's property to creditors.
6. Conveying a portion of the Company's estate at Hartlepool to the London and North-Western Railway Company.
7. Conveying lands purchased with the Company's funds to Mr. R. W. Jackson without any declaration of trust on his part that he held the lands in trust for the use of the Company.
8. Permitting Mr. R. W. Jackson to draw out and use for his own purposes certain monies, the property of the Company on foot, of which the present directors assert Mr. Jackson to be their debtor to the amount of about £25,000.
9. Publishing false accounts with the view of concealing from the shareholders and creditors the true position of the Company's affairs.

Although Lord Donoughmore had promised that Jackson would be heard by the Committee, and he turned up for that purpose, they would not hear him but nevertheless made their adverse report on the Bill. Lord Donoughmore, on presenting it, moved:

That the Report and Evidence be referred to Her Majesty's Attorney General, with Directions to inquire into the alleged illegal conduct of the late Directors and Auditors of the Company, and to institute a Prosecution against such Persons as, in his Opinion, can be convicted of illegal or fraudulent Conduct.

He said he felt he shouldn't be doing his duty if he did not call the attention of the House to some of the facts disclosed by the evidence taken before the Select Committee. He was "astonished to find that Mr. Sturge had failed to discover the facts although he had had an opportunity of examining the books". Referring to the proposals in the Bill, he went so far as to say – "This has ceased to be a question of rearrangement of capital. This is a case in which fraud and illegality are imputed, it is a case for which there exists no precedent and, I feel that if the Bill passes at all, it should pass on public grounds, and not as the act of a Committee of five Peers appointed to treat a mere private question". He admitted that if the Bill did not pass great loss and even ruin would follow to innocent parties. But, on the other hand, it would be unwise to allow the directors of public companies, who had been guilty of gross mismanagement, to feel that they had nothing to do but come before Parliament to make an appeal *ad misericordiam* in order to undo all the fraudulent acts they had done in the past, and thus encourage others to pursue the same course. The creditors of the Company were alone worthy of relief.

The Lord Chancellor said that the evidence given to the Select Committee, would, as a matter of course, be carefully investigated and considered by the Treasury solicitors, and if it appeared that an indictable offence had been committed, proceedings would be taken against the offenders. On this assurance Lord Donoughmore withdrew his motion and it was agreed that the Bill should be referred to the same Select Committee with Instructions to consider and Report whether the Bill might be allowed to proceed with a view of affording relief to the Bond-holders and Shareholders "not implicated in the illegal proceedings brought under the notice of the House, without exempting those Persons who may have been parties to those Proceedings from any responsibility they may thereby have incurred."

In making these harsh comments, it seems clear that Lord Donoughmore and his committee had accepted Coleman's evidence, and had heard no refutation of it, because Jackson had not been a petitioner in support of the Bill and, consequently, had not been heard. The fact that no prosection was instituted and that the Bill was allowed to pass without further strictures when the Select Committee reassembled, may be taken as the best evidence that no criminal fraud had been committed by Jackson.

(iv) On the 12th of June, 1872, Vice-Chancellor Malins gave his judgment in an action in the Chancery Court by the North Eastern Railway Company against Robinson Watson, in which the issue was whether Jackson was entitled to £26,250 Ordinary Consolidated Stock which had been registered in his name in circumstances earlier described. He found that Jackson was entitled to retain the stock and criticised the Plaintiffs for alleging fraud on the part of Jackson in this matter. He said the fact that there had never been any attempt to conceal the registration of the stock in the company's accounts and records, completely disposed of any suggestion of fraudulent intent.

(v) As earlier mentioned, the Court of Chancery had eventually found that Jackson had, without legal or proper authority, been credited with some £21,000, and they allowed the North Eastern Railway to surcharge the accounts to this extent.

In the light of all this it seems fair to say that:

(a) Jackson's acquisition of the steamboats and collieries was done without any intention of fraud or personal gain (except in so far as the success and growth of the West Hartlepool harbour and town would bring prosperity to Jackson personally).

(b) Jackson acted generally in the interests of West Hartlepool and its port, and was so dedicated to these interests that he took little account of rules and regulations, but had no intent, or expectation of defrauding those from whom he borrowed money to finance the undertaking.

(c) Jackson, in crediting himself with the two sums of £8,000 and other sums making a total of £21,000, no doubt thought that it was no more than a modest and just reward for his enterprise and skill, and, considering the size of the undertaking, many might have agreed with him.

(d) Jackson's bookkeeping, and failure to comply with company law and practice, was typical of his attitude to West Hartlepool generally. He knew he had founded and weaned the place, and he viewed it as his own, to be managed as he thought best. In this attitude he was not actuated by any intention to defraud; he always expected to succeed.

His character defects seem to have been – recklessness, a touch of megalomania, a facility for self-deception and self-justification (often giving the appearance of hypocrisy), a tendency to be side-tracked from what should have been his main objective, and, surprisingly in view of his achievements, a lack of vision. His obsession with the Christ Church affair was a demonstration of the penultimate defect and his persistence in advocating the harbour of refuge when ordinary foresight would have warned that the day of the sailing ship was rapidly coming to an end, is indicative of the last. It is, however, an interesting, if not improving reflection that had he not possessed at least some of these "defects", West Hartlepool might never have been created.

Is it true, as has been generally assumed, that Coleman's campaign did great harm to the prospects of West Hartlepool? Martin says (p. 44) – "In our opinion, had Mr. Benjamin Coleman never existed West Hartlepool would have been a much larger and important town than it is today." Robert

Wood says that, on amalgamation with the North Eastern Railway, "the glory had departed!" But what prospect really lay before the West Hartlepool Harbour and Railway Company if Jackson had been able to avoid Coleman? How long could he have gone on borrowing money to pay interest on capital already borrowed and, at the same time, develop the dock and harbour system to try to reach his dream goal? How long could he have gone on subsidising the steamboats and collieries, in the hope that the trade of the port could be increased sufficiently to enable him to put them on a paying basis? And what chance was there of the dream of creating on the east coast "a Port of Liverpool" ever being realised?

The answer must surely be that there never was any prospect of West Hartlepool, or, indeed, of any other port on the north east coast rivalling in size and importance the port of Liverpool. The conditions in north-east England were quite different from those on Merseyside and in Lancashire. The huge imports of cotton and other goods from the booming United States of America, the immense exports of manufactured goods from Lancashire, the great passenger traffic with Ireland and the United States, could never have been equalled, or even approached by the coal exports of Durham and Yorkshire, the trickle of passengers from Europe and the relatively small imports from the Continent. And, although West Hartlepool was the best port on the north-east coast for turn-round of ships, it was remote from the main centres of population and had no great manufacturing industries, except shipbuilding. Any trade with the Continent had to be won in competition with other ports all down the east coast, including the largest port of all, London.

The railway mania really was a mania. Lines were being developed with breakneck speed in places where they could never pay. There was a general lunacy in the railway world that spurred on more and more development in the vain hope that a monopoly of traffic might be secured and thus large fortunes made. Most of this was delusion.

As it turned out, Ralph Ward Jackson achieved a near

miracle. Entering the race when all others had travelled far, he managed to build a traffic which exceeded that of all the neighbouring ports. He brought a large share of the country's timber imports to West Hartlepool and Hartlepool. He made the coal exports compare with those of the old-established coal ports of the Tyne and Wear. He attracted shipowners until the port ranked fourth in the United Kingdom for Registered Shipping Tonnage and he provided the site for what became the most productive shipyards in the country. It is true that he did most of this by contriving illusions and by subsidising traffic in a way which could not have gone on for ever. But he did it, and, having done it, most of the trade and commerce did not go away when the game was up.

And as for the take-over by the North Eastern Railway surely that was the best thing that could have happened, for they were able to, and presently did, develop the port by building three more docks, additional timber ponds and warehouses, and an improved entrance to a unified harbour and dock system which was the most extensive on the north-east coast, including Hull. Their flat rate for the conveyance of timber made the port the largest importer of pit props in the country. If there had been the slightest chance of Jackson's dream being fulfilled, the North Eastern Railway would have been needed to do it.

As for the deluded bond and debenture holders of the West Hartlepool Harbour and Railway Company and its predecessors, they came out of it far better than they could have dared to hope, if they had known the truth when they lent their capital.

And as for Jackson himself, well, he didn't make a lot of money, but his name and fame became immortal. And, to Hartlepudlians, so they should be!

Appendix

Ralph Ward Jackson's Letter to *The Times* of the 8th September, 1863.

WEST HARTLEPOOL

To the Editor of *The Times*.

Sir, – My name, in connexion with the West Hartlepool Harbour and Railway undertaking, and the recent special report by Lord Donoughmore to the House of Lords, having been several times prominently adverted to in your powerful journal, I rely upon your known impartiality to give this letter a place in your columns. I am the more induced to trouble you at this time from the able remarks contained in *The Times* of the 27th of August last, and especially from the concluding observations, which appropriately suggest that, while the Select Committee of the House of Lords may not have had time to report on the extensive question of restricting companies from expending funds for purposes not specifically authorised by their Acts of Parliament, yet, "perhaps an impression prevailed that a certain discretion must be allowed to directors", that "there is no doubt it has been largely exercised, for railway companies have bought land, built hotels, and sometimes even purchased steamboats without Parliamentary powers", that, while "their operations ought to be vigilantly watched, Parliament, in turn, will do well to take into account the unforeseen emergencies of new and experimental undertakings", and that "a rigid limitation of the power of directors may, in some cases, be necessary for public purposes, but it would by no means uniformly promote the interests of shareholders."

To such liberal sentiments and practical views there can be but one general assent; and because they so directly apply to the special case of West Hartlepool I ask the favour of your allowing me, under all the circumstances, to give to these few observations of mine the like publicity as adverse comments on the subject have previously received in *The Times*.

In the many trying, extensive, and difficult matters I have had to contend with and overcome for West Hartlepool before the whole undertaking could be brought to the extent and completeness it now boasts of, I am not insensible that in the progress of accomplishing such a work, extending over years of intense anxiety and labour, some errors of judgment may have occurred – as in what new and great undertaking has there not been? – which are open to fair public criticism.

But I repel, with deep and natural indignation, any charge of fraud or personal corruption, or that I have on any occasion shown the smallest desire or done any one act unduly to benefit myself or any relative or friend throughout the period of the 25 years during which I have been arduously and faithfully engaged in the concerns of the West Hartlepool Harbour and Railway undertaking.

West Hartlepool, with its fine harbour, docks, warehouses, and town, situate on the west shore of Hartlepool Bay was, in 1844, an open beach, skirted by sandhills, and behind this desert ridge was an open agricultural country. A solitary farmhouse and a windmill were the only indications of human life and industry that marked the spot. In 1844 there were no works of any kind, no capital, no shipping, no commerce, – where are now the crowded thoroughfares, the overflowing emporium, the busy port.

In the International Exhibition of 1862 I exhibited a large model of West Hartlepool, the youngest seaport of the United Kingdom. The superficial area represented on the model was about 300 acres. The history in brief which was placarded on the case in which the model was enclosed, may yet be read and the model inspected at the Crystal Palace, Sydenham, and the placard gives the following facts to the end of 1861:– That in June, 1847, the harbour of 12 acres and the first (coal) dock of eight acres were opened, and that the harbour has been since enlarged to 44 acres. In June, 1852, the second (merchandise) dock of 14 acres was opened; also No. 1 graving dock 350ft. long. In June, 1857, the third (merchandise) dock of 10 acres was opened; also No. 2 graving

dock, 350ft. long; that timber dock and timber ponds, cover-
ing a water area of 24 acres and timber yards of upwards
of 20 acres have since been provided; that the new extensive
warehouses comprise a floor area of 13 acres, and upwards of
25 miles of railway are laid down for traffic approaches and
accommodation to the docks; that the area occupied by these
works alone is 245 acres, and ships of 2,000 tons and upwards are easily accommodated; that in 1847 the number of
ships entering was 460, and 5,964 in 1861; in 1847 the coal
shipped was 54,202 tons, and 975,319 tons in 1861; in
1853 the foreign merchandise exports commenced from the
manufacturing districts via West Hartlepool, and the returns
of Her Majesty's Customs were £23,846, in the year ending
December, 1853, and, £5,929,909 in the year 1861; that the
foreign imports also commenced in 1853, consisting of grain
16,750 qrs. in 1853 and 204,724 qrs. in 1861; flax and hemp
– 901 tons in 1853 and 4083 tons in 1861; timber – 531 tons
in 1853 and 57,250 tons in 1861; general goods – 4,885 tons
in 1853 and 19,446 tons in 1861; and that in 1847 the population of the district forming the new town of West Hartlepool
did not exceed 300 persons, but in 1861 numbered 14,000.

The population of West Hartlepool is now increased to
16,000, and in all other respects the indications of a progressive
increase of trade and of industrial success are unmistakably
exhibited. Indeed, such is the increase still going on in the
foreign (import) trade alone – especially in grain and timber –
that it was stated in evidence last Session by the present directors that additional warehouse and storage accommodation
are immediately required at a further expenditure of £80,000 or
£100,000; and this, let it be borne in mind, beyond all the
outlay in the time of the late directors. And, while the
annual revenue of the company was in 1852 only some
£80,000, it had risen to upwards of £216,000 in 1861, and is
still increasing. The revenue for the first two weeks in this
month of August is upwards of £11,900 and the recent evidence
of the present directors before Parliament shows that in
another year, such will be the income of the company, that,

after satisfying all preferential claims and agreed interest on debt, the ordinary stock of the company may expect a dividend of at least near 3 per cent.

This is the West Hartlepool which was, in certain quarters, recently denounced as "a bubble and a fraud", a place and a work not existing previous to June, 1847, but which, before I retired from the direction in April, 1862, had risen to be the fourth port in the United Kingdom for foreign merchandise exports – Liverpool being first, London second, Hull third and West Hartlepool fourth; and the Board of Trade Department of Her Majesty's Government had also announced in a public document to Parliament in the Session of 1861, West Hartlepool to be of "national importance." Previous to and during the recent legislation, now happily concluded, statements were put forth that would almost have led the uninformed public to believe that the capital which had been expended on producing these results had been hopelessly sunk in some hidden folly, or squandered in the personal delectation of some unknown adventurer.

I and the late directors acted upon the necessary policy of executing and bringing to completion, as quickly as possible, such a comprehensive system and extent of harbour and docks accommodation as would establish for the undertaking a character for shipping capacity and facilities such as would ensure for West Hartlepool, though the youngest port in the country, a position and prominence not inferior to any other shipping place on the North-east coast, it being obvious that, in a totally new creation such as West Hartlepool is, success would best and most surely be realised by making the harbour and docks and every requisite arrangement for shipping and commercial enterprise as comprehensive and perfect as practicable, and in the shortest time. It will readily be admitted that, towards making known and promoting the development of an entirely new port, formed where previously existed neither population, capital nor commerce, the company as the first settlers, and also in their character as carriers, are called upon in the infancy of such an undertaking, to initiate and encourage by pecuniary assistance and otherwise, many objects which in an old-established town or commercial locality are not so necessary. A less outlay or a longer period occupied in executing the works would not have answered the purpose, but have been more costly in the end, and would not have told in favour of the character and rapid development of the port of West Hartlepool, as experience and the returns now attest.

The first Act of Parliament for West Hartlepool was passed in 1844, the first works consisted of a small tidal harbour of twelve acres, and the dock of eight acres for shipping coal; and these were commenced in 1845, and opened on the 1st of June, 1847. The model and the statistical table referred to describe the various subsequent and extensive works and trade.

By virtue of an Act in 1852, this Harbour and Dock Company became amalgamated with two old railway companies, leading into the heart of the great South Durham coal field; and hence the three companies and the three undertakings became united into one company, under the present title, "The West Hartlepool Harbour and Railway Company."

One of the two old railway companies takes date from the year 1828, another from 1839, and the Harbour and Dock Company from 1844; and there is no doubt that the various Acts of Parliament relating to each, both prior and subsequent to their amalgamation in 1853 were, previous to the legislation in the Session just passed, open to considerable latitude of construction. The shareholders, and former boards of directors, in desiring to bring West Hartlepool and the whole undertaking as rapidly as possible to their present extent and completeness, felt themselves entitled to put such a liberal interpretation on the company's powers for capital and outlay as they considered, and were advised, the Acts and the company's true commercial interests would warrant.

By the Act of 1852 the capitals of the three companies were united, and, in addition to and plus all their loans, debts, and engagements, the amalgamated company were empowered to raise on loan one-third of their share capital for the time being, on one-half of it being paid up, which has always been the case, and has so appeared year by year in the company's balance sheets and books. As has been the case with other companies, of which, by reason of numerous amalgamations, and the introduction into their codes of the respective Acts of other companies, the limits of their loan and share capital have been brought to an indefinite condition until regulated by some consolidated Financial Act. So it was with the West Hartlepool Company and its component companies until by the legislation of 1863 the proportions of loan and share capital, by the consent of all creditors and shareholders, have been brought within the more recent rules of Parliamentary requirements.

Supposing even that in the great and unexpected exigencies for providing for the rapid and extraordinary increase of trade and shipping to West Hartlepool and the construction of difficult and untried harbour and sea works, the company to some extent exceeded what, under the strictures of adverse constructions of the Acts of Parliament, might be considered the extreme limit for borrowed monies, still the present directors even have proved, in evidence before Parliament, that the company possess, in surplus investments, securities, and properties, full value for all the money raised and expended beyond that which had been laid out by former directors on the harbour, docks, and railway works, all admitted to be for the real benefit of the company and those interested in its success and security.

Several additional directors, specially representing bond-holders, were appointed by the shareholders in February, 1862, and I continued to act with them until the following April, when from feelings of honour which I entertained that the new directors should have the most unrestricted and unbiassed means of investigating in their own way everything relating to the conduct and affairs of the company from the earliest period, I deemed it right to retire at that time from official connexion with the direction of the company's affairs.

Consequent upon the rapid expenditure of capital in the construction and perfecting of the great works of West Hartlepool as well as the originating and developing its vast trade, it became desirable to rearrange the capital, liabilities, and financial position of the company, while further outlay was also requisite to meet the pressure of increasing trade. Questions arose in the early part of 1862 between the creditors and shareholders of the company, and between the bond-holders themselves, as to their respective positions and priori-ties. Though no one doubted the real value and soundness of the undertaking, or that by giving it reasonable time for further development it would prove adequate and fairly remunerative for all investments in it, yet it was deemed proper, in order to avoid intermediate litigation and disputes, that application should be made to Parliament for an Act to define and consolidate the whole share and loan capital of the company, and settle the proportions and priorities of all investors.

Hence, a Bill was introduced into Parliament in the last Session which, after being fully discussed before a Select Committee of the House of Commons, was unanimously passed by that branch of the Legislature. The Bill then came before the House of Lords, and was referred to a Select Committee, of which the Earl of Donoughmore became chair-man.

Here arose the first real difficulties, the first real danger to the measure, and thence the official allegations which for a time gave to the matter so painful a notoriety. The Lords' Committee rejected the Bill, and Lord Donoughmore presented a long special report to the House of Lords which, while assigning no reasons whatever for throwing out the Bill, hypothetically assumed facts, confessedly made on *ex parte* statements and on data which don't exist. It also contained throughout personal reflections upon myself and others connected with the former management of the company, all of which occurred in our absence, and after, as I shall now show, I had offered myself to be examined, but was un-fortunately refused.

The Committee adjourned for the Whitsuntide recess, and, having heard that during the previous discussions *ex parte* statements and expressions had been made of a character personal to myself, I immediately wrote to Lord Donoughmore on the subject, and hence the correspondence which took place between me and his Lordship previous to this special report, and which is appended to it.

In the course of that correspondence Lord Donoughmore intimated what were the allegations suggested against me. These, it will be seen, I promptly and completely answered, and expressed myself ready and anxious to give any further explanation required on any and every point. In accordance, also, with the arrangement made with Lord Donoughmore, I went from the North of England expressly to attend the Committee on the 1st of June, on its reassembling, and I then presented myself to be heard and examined, but which, I regret to say, was not allowed, Lord Donoughmore announcing to me that the only reason for not hearing me was because "the matter the Committee had to decide upon was not my conduct as a director of the company, but whether the Bill should pass or not, that the statements with regard to my conduct only came out collaterally, and the Committee would not go into any evidence about it", yet, on the report being published, it was found to be altogether silent as to the reasons for rejecting the Bill – which had, in fact, become an entirely unopposed Bill – but contained throughout personal attacks and observations upon myself and others in the previous management of the company.

This state of things, then, led to two important but separate steps being taken – the one by myself and the other by the present directors. The first was a letter from me to Lord Donoughmore on the 6th of June last, pointing out the injustice of the special report as regards myself, and intimating my intention to present a petition to the House of Lords on the subject; the second was a petition by the present directors, supported by petitions from bondholders and shareholders, entreating the House of Lords, under the circumstances of the case, to recommit the Bill, with the view of its being passed into an Act this year.

These petitions were accordingly presented to the House of Lords on the 23rd. of June – mine by Lord Ravensworth, and the directors' by Lord Chelmsford. My petition set forth the matters contained in my correspondence with Lord Donoughmore. It adverted to my having answered every point and allegation made by Lord Donoughmore in his Lordship's letters, to my having urged upon him that, on the Committee re-assembling after the Whitsuntide recess, I might be allowed to be examined to give any further explanation which might be required of me; to my having expressly and indignantly denied that I had ever been a party to the conversion to my own use of one farthing of the company's funds; to my having, on the contrary, a considerable balance justly due to me from the company; to my having repeatedly offered to the present directors to refer any matters of account between us to arbitration, but without success; to my having denied in the most earnest and emphatic manner that on any occasion I had been a party to the publication of false accounts of the company's affairs; to the facts that the company possess about a million in value of surplus properties and assets, yet to be realised, over and above the outlay apportioned for the undertaking and works; and that there is a large excess of receipts over expenditure on revenue accounts, with every prospect of increase under energetic and proper management, and the putting an end to litigation.

The petition of the present directors complained of the hardship to the company and to the bondholders and shareholders, who were almost universally agreed on all points, in being prevented from securing the re-arrangement of their investments, and of the general financial affairs of the company, and prayed that the Bill might be re-committed to another Committee, in the hope of its being allowed to pass into an Act this year; and the present directors urged that "the great importance of the port of West Hartlepool furnishes a further and public ground for saving it by the passing of the Bill, and that there are abundant public reasons for knowing the Board of Trade Department of Her Majesty's Government consider the upholding of the port of West Hartlepool to be a matter of national importance".

The result of all this was that the re-committal of the West Hartlepool Bill became a public question, and the House of Lords, to their honour, regarding both sets of petitions, after some conversation, referred the subject and the Bill to another Select Committee, composed of 15 members of their Lordships' House, and who on the 30th of June, without calling upon counsel, or for any other evidence, or requiring any further explanation from me, passed the Bill, which received the Royal Assent on the 13th of July last.

The Donoughmore report had meantime, on his Lordship's motion, been ordered to be printed, and shortly afterwards the evidence upon which the report purported to have been based was also printed, and the attention of the British Press was directed to the subject. So far as I have been able to discover, the text (with a few exceptions) upon which many talented writers on the subject descanted was Lord Donoughmore's report to the House of Lords, not the evidence; and with this for the basis of their observations, the opinion expressed was, in effect, "Here is surely some great bubble and fraud. What is all this about?"

Journals which having also seen the evidence dwelt with emphasis on the fact that the Donoughmore report contained statements in some respects not founded upon the evidence at all, and in other respects not justified by it. One striking illustration of the report containing matter not founded on any evidence whatever before the Committee may be here introduced. Lord Donoughmore states, as implying a point of mis-management against the late directors, thus:−

"In one instance the directors are said to have taken an acceptance for £10,000 from a colliery owner in payment of railway and shipping dues owing by him. They afterwards endorsed the acceptance over to one of the company's creditors, the colliery owner has become insolvent, and the company is now liable as endorser of the acceptance."

From what source and how such an allegation appears in the report is most mysterious, for, throughout the whole of the evidence, there is not only not one syllable to support it, but I maintain no such transaction ever occurred in the affairs of the company, nor anything approaching or giving the slightest colour to it. *Ex uno disce omnes.**

I submit that from an unfortunate misapprehension of facts and imperfect evidence the Donoughmore report is erroneous in several respects. It assumes the present company to be a newly-constituted company, and the undertaking a new work, originating with the year 1852, instead of, as it is, the consolidation of three old dissolved companies and three separate undertakings. It also assumes that the amalgamated company were limited as to their borrowed capital to one-third of the united share capital, whereas, at the very time of the amalgamation, the loans and the liabilities of the three companies confessedly exceeded considerably more than such one-third; and which loans and liabilities, being imposed upon and inherited by the united company could not, as indeed the Act did not prescribe that they should, form any part of the additional powers simultaneously conferred upon the amalgamated company for future loans for the future purposes and future outlay of that company. It further assumes that the borrowing powers under the Act of 1852 had not come into operation at all, or that they could not be exercised to the extent of one-third of the capital, because, it was assumed, the requisite amount of one half of the authorised share capital had not been paid up; whereas the fact is that more than the specified proportion of share capital was paid up, and so appeared in the company's books and in the accounts issued with the directors' report year by year to the proprietors. And the report also ignores the fact – expressly brought to Lord Donoughmore's knowledge by my previous letters to his Lordship – that when in the Session of 1861 the company had two Bills in Parliament – one for powers for

* From one judge all.

increased share and loan capital, and the other for securing
general traffic arrangements with other companies – the House
of Commons had yielded to the opposing parties, and inserted
in one of the Bills a clause to limit the borrowed monies
of the amalgamated company to one-third of the share capital;
but the House of Lords actually struck out that clause on its
being clearly demonstrated to them that according to the fair
construction of all the Acts together, the united company
were not so restricted.

Previously to this decision, eminent equity and common law
counsel had been also referred to, and a case laid before
them, together with all the company's Acts of Parliament, to
advise as to the company's securities; and, after a careful
examination of the Acts and all the circumstances, the counsel
gave their joint opinion, "That all the company's bonds and
mortgage debentures, either within or exceeding one-third of
the share capital of the company, were good and binding
securities at law and in equity, and for which the undertaking
and properties of the company were liable," and all this I
stated to Lord Donoughmore in my correspondence previous
to his report.

The Act of Parliament, however, now passed dissipates
and settles all doubts and questions on the subject, and confirms the whole capital, securities, and outlay of the company
under all former directors.

In the same Session (1861), and during the same inquiry
before Parliament, the published summaries of the company's
accounts and the reports of the directors for several years
were produced and scrutinized, and I was fully examined upon
them by the counsel of parties who had antagonistic and
competing interests to West Hartlepool, and were more or less
ranged in formidable array against the company's two Bills,
and desirous of checking the progress of their young and enterprising neighbour, the port of West Hartlepool.

The result, however, was the passing of those Bills, the conferring upon the company further powers for share and loan
capital, and the expression of the opinion by the select

Ralph Ward Jackson's statue in front of the east end of Christ Church.

The presentation portrait of Ralph Ward Jackson painted by Francis Grant, R.A., in 1855.

committee of the House of Commons that while I had, no doubt, shown an extreme zeal and enthusiasm for West Hartlepool and the company's works and interests, "the committee did not attach to him in any shape any criminality, nor that he had done anything for his own personal benefit." The same committee added they "deemed it right, in justice to Mr. Ward Jackson's character, to state that," and the counsel for the opponents immediately and handsomely expressed their entire assent to that sentiment and declaration.

In my correspondence with Lord Donoughmore it will be seen I referred to this circumstance; and it is, therefore, additionally to be regretted that his Lordship did not do me the justice to hear me, when the same explanations, with no doubt the same result, would have occurred, and thus no such assumptions and no personal imputations could have found a place in Lord Donoughmore's report.

It is, however, fair to say that his Lordship, when assuming erroneous publications of accounts, appears to have been misled by certain *ex parte* comparative statements which were furnished to him. But on a recent impartial examination of these by a public accountant of Newcastle-on-Tyne with the books and balance sheets of the company those statements are found to be mere manipulations, or transpositions of figures, taken from one common and agreed source – viz., the books and office balance sheets of the company, which are on all hands and in evidence admitted to have been "well" and "truly kept", and "in a manner which may be understood by any person of ordinary capacity". The compiler of those comparative statements for Lord Donoughmore not only did not follow the same phraseology of items adopted by the late directors in their published summaries of accounts, but he aggregated in one sum, and under one head, by a different language, items that in the late directors' summaries are to be found and referred to in several sums. Hence the apparent discrepancies – though, on reference to the detailed balance sheets and books there is no difference at all in the totals.

I may illustrate by a few instances the errors into which

Lord Donoughmore had – of course inadvertently – by this means been drawn. Firstly, by the incompleteness, on the one hand, of those *ex parte* comparative statements; secondly, by the unfortunate refusal to allow me, on the other hand, to be examined and explain. Lord Donoughmore selected the accounts in December, 1860, and stated that, while the ordinary or consolidated stock amounted to £287,878, the late directors published £815,853. Now the fact is, the item in the late directors' "summary" of accounts expressed this item thus, – "Receipts on account of ordinary stock and advances convertible into consolidated stock issued, £815,853", whereas the compiler of the comparative statement furnished to Lord Donoughmore (and, of course, his Lordship knew nothing personally of the matter), avoided all mention of the "and advances convertible into consolidated stock issued," and this made all the difference.

In like manner Lord Donoughmore was misled when stating the money borrowed on debenture loans to be £2,520,013, but, according to the late directors, £671,520, the facts being that in respect of that debenture loan account the comparative statement includes in it several hundred thousand pounds more than is warranted by the evidence actually given before the committee, and the compiler had also included under the one head of "debenture loan account" not only the "advances convertible into consolidated stock issued" and the £671,520, but also various miscellaneous items of unsecured current accounts, the cost and balance in respect of the company's surplus lands and houses, and other sums, all of which are specified and referred to in the late directors' summary under several heads.

There was no evidence whatever given before the committee as to the late "directors diminishing the true amount of their expenditure upon works by nearly £130,000", as assumed in Lord Donoughmore's report, and there is nothing of the sort in the books and balance-sheets of the company.

Lastly, Lord Donoughmore had also been misled when stating that the late directors "admit debts to be due to them for £485,115, while the true amount is £778,190", for the compiler of the comparative statement had, using his own phraseology for the item, in "debts due to the company, £778,190. 16s. 10d.", unfairly included with the £485,115 three other sums of £58,179, £40,640 and £194,256, – the first being shares held by the company in the Cleveland Railway, the second being also shares in the North Eastern Railway, and the third being "amounts owing to the company on current accounts", all of which are referred to and appear properly under other and separate items and balances in the late directors' published summary of account. Similar explanations apply to all the other comparative statements for previous years furnished to Lord Donoughmore.

Hence, it is the more unfortunate that I, whose volunteering and entreating to explain and be examined before Lord Donoughmore's committee, should have been refused. Had I been so examined it may be fairly concluded that the painful misunderstanding and the severe observations which have appeared, would have been altogether obviated.

But, after all, I recur with pleasure, which I know to be almost universal in the north of England, to the important fact of the company's Bill having ultimately become an Act of Parliament in the last Session, resulting from the fairness and justice of the House of Lords.

The report of the present directors, with the capital and revenue accounts to the 30th of June, 1863, was submitted to the proprietors at the half-yearly general meeting on the 24th of August last. The directors appropriately observe that "few other instances are to be found where the House of Lords has consented to reverse the decision of a committee upon a private Bill," and pleasingly conclude by stating, "that as regards both its capital and expenditure, the company is now entirely relieved from its embarrassment," and that "its present sound financial position affords a guarantee to the trading interests and the public that the great natural advantages of the port of West Hartlepool will now be fully developed."

The directors show the income for the half-year to the 30th of June last to be £109,257. 5s. 5d., and the net increase on the half year's revenue operations to be £15,506. 1s. 8d. over the corresponding period in 1862, and they also refer with satisfaction to the conversion, by virtue of the Act just passed, of the debenture and other debts of three old companies and the amalgamated company into share capital, by which, added to the previous issued and paid-up shares of upwards of £1,000,000, the company now possess a Parliamentary paid-up share capital of £3,000,000, with power to raise in addition £1,000,000 by new loans; and, for this the directors confidently urge that the West Hartlepool undertaking "affords a security in no respect inferior to that of any railway company."

All this confirms what was published in February, 1862, by a circular issued by a committee of large and influential bondholders and shareholders, who had met in London to consider a re-arrangement of the financial position of the company, and which I and the late directors had recommended. That committee, in suggesting measures to be adopted – and which embraced the application to Parliament for the purpose – stated that they were "glad to say they have obtained the concurrence of the (late) directors, as well as the approval of several large shareholders" in the measures proposed, and "in the meantime beg to express a confident belief that the undoubted resources of the company may be so developed and its affairs so conducted as to insure the ultimate discharge of every obligation".

It is, therefore, a most gratifying *finale* that all the steps taken in ultimately securing the capital Act of the last Session have resulted in the complete re-establishment of the company's financial position; in the adoption and confirmation by Parliament of all the works, capital, and outlay of the amalgamated company, and of the three component companies from their earliest formation; in the admission that all the moneys raised have been fully accounted for and laid out for the real benefit and promotion of the undertaking and the interests of the shareholders and bondholders; and in the fact that, in all essential points, the present directors are adopting and continuing the works and policy in regard to the undertaking and West Hartlepool which their predecessors had boldly and honestly established.

I now hope that all feelings of asperity or jealousy, wherever entertained, will henceforth be dispelled, and that all the directors, bondholders, and shareholders will unite and cordially act together to promote and work out this important undertaking, and crown it with that signal success which, by its nautical position, soundness and capabilities, it is eminently calculated to attain.

I regret the intrusion of so long a letter in the valuable columns of *The Times*, but I felt that I could not do myself and the subject justice by curtailing it, the subject being, moreover, an illustration, in some respects, of the principles set forth in the observations I have taken the liberty to quote from the able article in *The Times* of the 27th of August.

I am, Sir, your very obedient servant,

RALPH WARD JACKSON

Greatham-hall, Aug. 31.

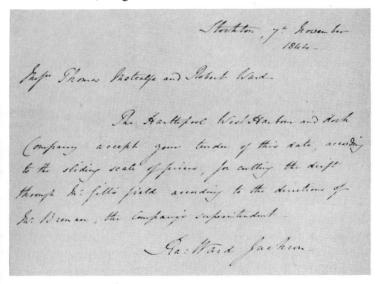

RALPH WARD JACKSON'S OBITUARY in the *South Durham and Cleveland Mercury* of the 14th August, 1880.

DEATH OF MR. RALPH WARD-JACKSON

The sad intelligence of the death of Mr. Ralph Ward-Jackson arrived too late for announcement in the principal part of our issue last week. Though we were aware that Mr. Jackson was ill, we had no idea that his sickness was unto death. It appears, however, that in the inner circle of his friends, the gravest anxiety had been felt for some days. The end came on Friday, the 6th inst., and a brilliantly useful, though for himself disastrous, career was thereby closed.

The late Mr. Ralph Ward-Jackson was the third son of William Ward Jackson, of Normanby Hall, North Yorkshire. He was born June 7, 1806, was educated at Rugby, and at the time of his death was in his 75th year. The Jacksons of Normanby are an ancient family, who trace their lineage up to a John Jackson, of Hickleton, one of the Knights of James I., and through him to the Ducketts, whose names occur with honour in English history as far back as the reign of Henry III. Port Jackson, in New South Wales, was named after one of his ancestors. The Ducketts were Royalists in the Civil Wars; but the Jacksons of Normanby were staunch Liberals. All the family were Liberals, including Mr. Ralph Ward-Jackson in his early years. One of his brothers (Mr. Edwin Ward-Jackson) stood as a candidate in the Liberal interest for a South Country borough, but unfortunately without success. Mr. Ralph Ward-Jackson's political opinions in these early days may be inferred from the fact that in the year 1852 he was strongly recommended as a Liberal candidate for South Durham by no less staunch a Radical than the late John Candlish in the columns of the Sunderland News. Mr. Jackson's falling away from the Liberal ranks was brought about when Mr. Farrer was member for South Durham, and the solicitors to the Eldon Trustees, Messrs. Bell, Steward, and Lloyd, acted as Parliamentary agents for the bills which he was promoting in connection with the West Hartlepool Railway Co. and the North Yorkshire and Cleveland Railway Co. At that time, however, Mr. Jackson showed no disposition to enter political life. His politics were summed up in the words "West Hartlepool". He was for West Hartlepool first, and for Whig or Tory afterwards all his life. Few more distinctively local men ever lived. Mr. Jackson, although so devoted to West Hartlepool was not born there. When he first saw the light, wild rabbits held possession of the site of what is now a great and thriving town. He was not a child of West Hartlepool. West Hartlepool was a child of his. He was born in Cleveland, began business in Stockton, and settled at Greatham. In 1829 he married Susanna, second daughter of Charles Swainson, of Cooper Hill, Lancashire, by whom he had issue one son, William Charles Ward-Jackson, who survives him. Mr. Jackson, having served articles at Preston, subsequently arranged a partnership with Mr. Frank, solicitor, Stockton, and in conjunction with him conducted for some years a considerable business. The law, however, had no great attractions for him. His mind dwelt upon the great possibilities in the way of commerce brought within reach by the construction of railways, the first of which had only a short while before been opened; and the first direct indication of his interest in this direction was given in the share he took in the establishment of the Stockton and Durham County Bank. The prospectus of this institution, established in 1838, stated that the opening out of various railways and branches, with the consequent increase of trade, called for an augmentation of banking facilities, and promised success – which statement was prefectly true, though the Stockton and Durham County Bank got none of the benefit. After eight years of unprofitable experience the business was transferred to the National Provincial, and the shutters put up. But Mr. Jackson had in the meanwhile, along with some of his colleagues in the banking business – Mr. Cuthbert Wigham and others – put his hand to a project which, mainly by his personal exertions, was carried to a more successful issue. This was the formation of the Stockton and

Hartlepool Railway Company, of which he became first the solicitor and afterwards the chairman.

The story of his early struggles is now well-nigh forgotten by all but his contemporaries. Other men have laboured and we have entered into their labours; and thousands in West Hartlepool today know little more than the man but for whom West Hartlepool would never have existed. He it was who first projected the idea of constructing a dock and harbour on what Mr. George Leeman once graphically described as the "blown sand hills" in the sheltered recess of the Hartlepool peninsula, and such was the animating energy which he devoted to that undertaking that in 1847 he had the gratification of seeing his labours crowned with success. The new harbour sent its thousands of tons of South Durham coals to distant marts from the close of that year and only three more summers had succeeded when the trade established by the first enterprise was quadrupled in amount, while additional works were completed which cast into shade the first efforts of the West Hartlepool Company. Rivalries and oppositions innumerable had been opposed or overcome in order to the attainment of these; and those best acquainted with the hidden history of the difficulties which beset each successive undertaking confess, in words once used by Mr. Leeman, that "one man only was found competent to the task, and to him we owe everything – Ralph Ward Jackson." When Mr. Jackson first connected the towns of Stockton and Hartlepool by the new railway, Hartlepool had not long ceased to be a fishing village and watering-place. The opening of the Old Hartlepool railways, tapping the Ferryhill and Hartlepool colliery district, had led to the creation of a new port on the east coast. The success of the Dock and Harbour Railway Company, of which Mr. Rowland Burdon and Mr. Thomas Wood were leading directors, stimulated Mr. Jackson to undertake a similar enterprise. If it had not been for the obstructive policy of the old company, which positively discouraged the shipping of coal from new districts in their dock, no independent port might have been created. The Clarence Railway, with which the Stockton and

Hartlepool was identified, tapped the Coxhoe district, and they looked upon it with jealousy and suspicion. They did not encourage his enterprise, and, as a consequence, he was forced to resort to his original plan, and start a dock and harbour at West Hartlepool. His success was great and almost immediate. In 1847, the harbour was opened, and in 1851 it had already displayed such signs of vigour that a magnificent piece of plate was presented to Mr. Jackson by the merchants, shipowners, tradesmen, and others residing in West Hartlepool, in recognition of his services in creating the port. In 1852 the second dock was opened, and in 1855, the town still growing apace, his portrait, painted by Francis Grant, R.A., was presented to the Commissioners in trust for the town on Oct. 2nd. 1855. The presentation was made by Mr. George Leeman, whose approaching retirement from the chairmanship of the North Eastern Board was made public within a few hours of Mr. Jackson's death. The day was kept as a public holiday in the town, and on the occasion of the presentation, Mr. Jackson made a speech recounting the successive stages of his labours on behalf of the town which, from the autobiographical details will be read with interest to-day. Mr. Jackson said:

"The first work in the south of the County of Durham in which I took an interest was the construction of the Stockton and Hartlepool Railway, the object of which was to connect the Clarence Railway with Hartlepool. The port of Hartlepool had become a little prominent by reason of the success of the works projected by the Dock and Railway Company. Great credit was due to them for their enterprise, they brought it to a considerable point of success, and parties connected with the Clarence Railway said it would be to their interest to take advantage of the port of Hartlepool. I was spoken to on the subject, and having a strong fancy for the sea, and also a great liking for engineering, and above all a great desire to have something to do with old Neptune and Boreas, I took it in hand. Opposition was threatened to the formation of this connecting line between Clarence and Hartlepool, and I then conceived the idea of forming this line without an Act of Parliament and by perseverance it was accomplished. (*Loud cheers.*) It is not general, but in that instance it was done, and was, in fact, the basis upon which the future establishment and present position of West Hartlepool stands. Unless that railway had been made, and that without an Act of Parliament, my belief is that we should never have been here enjoying ourselves this evening. (*Cheers.*) Having established the Stockton and Hartlepool Railway, the proposition was at an early period made to form an independent shipping place and arrangements were made with the Dock Company for the purpose of receiving coals shipped from the Stockton and Hartlepool Railway for a specific period on terms not considered very liberal; and it was therefore agreed that the period of shipping in the old dock should only be for three years, it being specially reserved that at the end of that period we should be at liberty to resort to our original plan – a dock and harbour of our own. (*Cheers.*) The Stockton and Hartlepool line was opened in 1841, and in 1844 I took the Bill into parliament for the formation of the West Harbour and the first dock; and eventually I overcame the opposition I there met with. That was in the autumn of 1845. In the spring of 1845 we turned the first sod at the back of some sand hills, and I well remember on that very day chasing a rabbit about the place with very great delight. In 1845 we began the first dock and harbour at West Hartlepool, and on the 1st of June, 1847, I had the pleasure of seeing the harbour opened and the dock as well. The area of both works was then only thirteen acres in the harbour and eight acres in the dock. In 1848 the proposition came before the public of connecting the town of Leeds with Hartlepool and Stockton, and I immediately foresaw the great importance of the connection, and urged upon the proprietors who had embarked their capital in the first harbour and dock the propriety of making provision for a larger dock accommodation, feeling quite certain that unless accommodation was provided we should never be in a situation to receive or expect it. The proprietors, with great liberality, allowed the second dock to be made, and that was opened on the 1st June, 1852. The Leeds line was very shortly afterwards completed, and the result has been of the most gratifying and satisfactory character. Not content with the second dock, but being rather ambitious of having one of the best ports on this side of the coast, I urged the formation of a third dock, and an additional graving dock to the one opened in 1853 – (*Cheers*) –, and I am confident that the advice I then gave will be found correct. When that dock, and the accommodation for timber, be completed, there will be the means of receiving a traffic at least double that of the present. Though the works now in formation are not double, yet the whole will be able to accommodate double what it does now. (*Hear, hear,*) In the course of the works, with the harbour especially, there has been a very great deal of intricacy. I have had to watch it carefully both night and day, and I believe very firmly we have succeeded in overcoming Old Neptune on the one hand and the sand on the other. (*Hear, hear.*) From a depth of water which I need not name here when we first opened, we have now very nearly no sand at all, and the works we are now doing in the harbour will be the means of entirely preventing all influx of sand or any accumulations whatever. From this place we are now enabled to send ships to sea with very great ease at 18 feet of water, and I have no hesitation in saying if that were generally known, we should never know the want of large ships. (*Hear, hear.*) The harbour of refuge has been the last work which has engaged my most special and earnest attention – (*hear, hear.*) – and no one knows how much has had to be endured and overcome in connection therewith as my friend in the chair (Mr. Geo. Leeman). It will not be necessary for me to point out the many difficulties I had to encounter, almost single-handed, in taking it through Parliament; but I may say it is one of the utmost importance to this district – (*hear, hear*) – far more so than many can at present say – not only as a work having for one of its objects the saving of our great sea lines, but also for being the means of producing such shipping accommodation in the Bay of Hartlepool as certainly cannot be produced, I say it unhesitatingly, on the whole of this coast. Before very long I hope we shall be able to open the third dock and the second graving dock, and the harbour of refuge, and when we have done that West Hartlepool will have been brought to a state of perfection never contemplated when I chased the rabbit at the commencement of the first dock. (*Cheers.*)

It was in the year 1852 when there was a great rejoicing at Stockton on the occasion of the opening of the Leeds Northern

Railway, bringing Stockton into direct communication with the West Riding, that he fixed upon the idea of making West Hartlepool the terminal port for lines of independent communication with the South. With this end in view he projected the North York and Cleveland Railway, which was by him carried as far as Stokesley, and afterwards completed by the North-Eastern Railway Company. His other bill for constructing the West Hartlepool and North Riding Railways was less successful. At first he proposed to cross the Tees on a bridge below Stockton, and in a subsequent session, by means of a steam ferry below Middlesbrough. Both schemes were objected to on account of the danger of interrupting the river navigation, and they were strongly opposed by the Stockton and Darlington Railway Company at the instance of the late Joseph Pease. The Stockton and Darlington Bill was carried, the West Hartlepool Bill was mutilated. The miserable remnant which ultimately received parliamentary sanction related to the construction of a shipping pier at Normanby. Mr. Jackson was more successful in his labours to improve, extend, and develop West Hartlepool. After the new harbour was made, he was much annoyed by its silting up with sand. He formed a theory as to how the sand could be washed out instead of being washed into the harbour, and to verify his theory he was wont to wade out into the sea up to his middle, with the characteristic self-devotion of a whole-minded enthusiast. At last he believed he hit upon the secret of success, and he constructed wave traps at the land end of the piers, by which the accumulation of sand was successfully overcome. Under the stimulus of Mr. Jackson's energy, West Hartlepool grew amain. Speaking in 1855 as to the rule by which he was guided he said with perfect truth:

"It has always been my endeavour to do justice and see that all interests were properly protected, and that each person who came to locate himself in the town should have full and fair scope for his enterprise."

It was no easy task. Nothing but an indomitable will and

an energy which never wearied would have carried him through all his difficulties. He said himself on one occasion:

> "I know that if I had been overwhelmed with the difficulties opposed to me during the last seven or eight years, I should have laid down and died – the work would never have been done. But I simply said, 'I want it doing. I will try to get it done', and it has been accomplished."

It was always "Try, try, and try again," with Mr. Jackson. No discouragement disheartened him. No reverse made him despair. Whenever he was thrown he always came up smiling. There was a store of inexhaustible pugnacity in the man which found abundant scope in wrestling first with Neptune and Boreas, and then with the North-Eastern Railway Company. He was never still. Always up and doing – with a heart for any fate – he merited a better fate than that which ultimately overtook him. It was the very unrestrainable energy of the man which led to the overstepping of the "narrow limits" within which he should have confined his steps, and to that cause were due the painful vicissitudes which characterised his later career. Mr. Jackson was a broad-spirited, liberal-minded man. Although a Churchman he was no bigot, and his antipathy to clerical ascendancy led him into more than one characteristic combat with the first Vicar of Christ Church, the Rev. John Burgess, now of Birmingham. Mr. Jackson was the patron of Christ Church, which he had in great measure built and endowed, but he differed from the incumbent as to the unsectarian character of the public schools which he founded at West Hartlepool, and a controversy arose which had as one of its incidents the violent bursting in of the church doors and the invasion of the sacred edifice by a disorderly crowd of sailors, roughs, loose women, and others, who are not usually to be found inside church doors. Tradition says that in the course of the shindy that ensued a graceless sailor climbed into the pulpit and smoked his pipe at his ease as he swung one leg over the side of the sacred rostrum. The episode was Jacksonian, and it had its origin in a healthy detestation of sectarian bigotry, which did him honour.

In those early days Mr. Jackson did everything. Whether it was a church, a lock-up, an Atheneum, or a cemetery, Mr. Ralph Ward-Jackson was always to the front. It was he who, in 1853, applied for the Town Improvement Act, which in June, 1854, received the Royal Assent. It was he who was first Commissioner. If there was anything that Mr. Jackson did not do, the West Hartlepool Dock Company did it; and the West Hartlepool Dock Company was usually only another name for Mr. Jackson. The Dock Company gave sites for everything that was charitable, and sold sites for everything that was useful. The Mechanics' Institute was established under the patronage of Mr. Jackson, in 1835; and the Atheneum was built chiefly by the Dock Company and Mr. Jackson in 1852. He was helper and promoter of every good work and in the most of it all he found time to worry Canon Tristram in the law courts, and to promote his grand idea of the creation of a Harbour of Refuge at the Hartlepools. The Harbour of Refuge Scheme was a fixed idea with Mr. Jackson. Lord Claud Hamilton and Sir John Pakington fooled him to the top of his bent, and no end of money was wasted in commissions and surveys and inquiries, which led to nothing. Lord Palmerston at last, aided by Mr. Wilson, afterwards Finance Minister for India, and Mr. Milner Gibson, settled the question by legislation under which all the great improvements on the Tyne and Tees have taken place, and more recently in the Hartlepools, by means of Government advances at low rates of interest on the security of works themselves.

Mr. Jackson was ever one of those who make their right hand help their left, and his restless energy, not exhausted by his manifold labours in founding a town, excavating docks, and promoting railways, sought to increase the prosperity of his harbour by extending the operations of the West Hartlepool Railway and Dock Co. – the Dock and Railway Co. having been amalgamated in 1853. He was supreme in the

Board of Directors, and under his auspices they began to extend their operations beyond the limits for which they had authorisation in their Acts of Parliament. To encourage trade, and to bring grist to their mill, they invested their capital in collieries, and to dispose of their coals they bought a fleet of steamers, and when they ran short of capital they borrowed money, and so kept the ball rolling to the great satisfaction of everyone at West Hartlepool for some time. But after this had gone on for many years, and West Hartlepool had become one of the most prosperous ports on the North East Coast, one Benjamin Coleman, a spiritualist stock and share broker, who had a small interest in the concern, began to poke his nose into the accounts of the Railway and Dock Company. He smelt a rat, and loudly proclaimed the fact far and near. He wrote pamphlets, he attacked the directorate, he agitated the matter, and at last the directors were compelled to consent to the appointment of a committee of investigation. The immediate result of the appointment of that committee was the suspension of the authority of the Board over which Mr. Jackson presided, and the promotion of a special Act of Parliament providing against the serious financial errors which had taken place and for the numerous proceedings *ultra vires* which had characterised the management of the company. When the bill was before the Committee of the House of Lords, Lord Donoughmore, the chairman, did all that he could to prevent Mr. Jackson being heard as a witness before the committee. The *Stockton and Hartlepool Mercury* having commented strongly upon the injustice of the attempt to deny Mr. Jackson a hearing, Lord Donoughmore lost his temper, and threatened to move that the publishers of the *Mercury* should be brought to the bar of the House for a breach of the privileges of the High Court of Parliament. The Lord Chancellor, interposing, secured a day's delay. The *Stockton and Hartlepool Mercury* repeated the offence, commenting vigorously on the double injustice to Mr. Jackson and to the *Mercury* of which Lord Donoughmore was guilty, but His Lordship prudently allowed his wrath to evaporate, and our local contemporary lost the chance of one of the best advertisements a newspaper can ever have.

While Mr. Jackson was dispossessed of authority, much to the indignation of the people of West Hartlepool, opinion was divided as to his conduct. Rowland Burdon was very harsh in the condemnation of Mr. Jackson. Local opinion, however, was strongly in his favour, and shortly afterwards, the Hartlepools being called upon to elect a member, they showed their appreciation of his services by returning him in spite of his politics as first member for the newly-enfranchised borough by a majority of seven. He held the seat for six years. In 1874 he was defeated by his former unsuccessful opponent, Mr. Richardson, by a large majority, and he did not again renew the attempt to gain Parliamentary honours. Misfortunes thickened around him in these later years. The North-Eastern Railway Company bought up the West Hartlepool Dock and Railway Company, and Mr. Jackson became involved in a protracted litigation, which continued till within a month or two of his decease. The spirit of the man never failed him, even in the long years of his adversity. This he showed by the tenacity with which he sought what he esteemed to be his rights as against the North-Eastern; and also by the energy with which he threw himself into new work. He devised a scheme for supplying Cheltenham with water, engaged in sundry coal speculations, and, as we know, has recently been devoting himself to plans for the improvement of the harbour at Whitby. Any notice of the life-work of Mr. Jackson is incomplete which fails to mention the care bestowed by him to provide for the great population he has brought together all the comforts and conveniences of civilised society. The institutions of West Hartlepool tell of his forethought, his breadth of sympathy, and his unbounded liberality.

BENJAMIN COLEMAN and SPIRITUALISM

Benjamin Coleman was a leading supporter of Spiritualism during its rise in popularity in Britain during the third quarter of the nineteenth century. His own account of his conversion to a belief in it was that, whilst living in "the village of Ealing" in 1855, he was a near neighbour of Mr. and Mrs. Rymer, at whose house Mr. Home, "the celebrated medium", was then living as one of the family and was giving demonstrations of psychic phenomena. Coleman heard of them and became interested. Shortly afterwards another medium from America, Mrs. Newton, came to the Rymers and held séances. Coleman attended some of them and said "I soon, through her brilliant exemplification, realised the wisdom of the Apostle Paul, when he says that 'God hath chosen the foolish things of the world to confound the wise, and the weak things of the world to confound the mighty'."

Never doing things by halves, Coleman, whilst conducting his actions against Edwin Ward Jackson and his campaign against Ralph Ward Jackson, also threw himself wholeheartedly into the support of Spiritualism, and became a regular contributor to, and financial backer of, the *Spiritual Magazine*. He also visited the United States in April, 1861, for the purpose of meeting leading Spiritualists and the best-known mediums of New York and Boston. On his return he wrote a small book entitled *Spiritualism in America*, which was published by F. Pitman, and contained numerous accounts of psychic phenomena.

In 1865 he wrote another booklet, *Scepticism and Spiritualism: the experiences of a Sceptic, etc.* This was followed in 1871 by *The Rise and Progress of Spiritualism in England*, a small volume consisting of articles which he had previously had published in Spiritualist magazines.

His strong support of Spiritualism involved him in criminal libel proceedings in 1866. Briefly, the circumstances were that a popular stage character actor and comedian, Mr. Sothern (appearing on the stage as "Lord Dundreary") had become interested in Spiritualism and had spent two years in America investigating its claims. He became convinced that it was being practised by impostors and, with a collaborator, organised séances in America and Britain at which he produced apparent psychic manifestations of the most astonishing kind, but shortly afterwards revealed that they had been performed by trickery. This infuriated the Spiritualists, and the New York *Sunday Times* published an article accusing Sothern of having raped a young actress while she was under mesmeric influence. Benjamin Coleman reproduced an extract from this article in the February, 1866, *Spiritual Magazine* and Sothern thereupon commenced criminal libel proceedings against both Coleman and the publishers of the magazine.

Before the action was commenced, and after the London *Times* had, at Sothern's request, withdrawn an advertisement of the *Spiritual Magazine*, Coleman had written a letter to *The Times* saying he was prepared to justify every word published in the *Spiritual Magazine* respecting Mr. Sothern.

The case against Coleman first came before the Deputy Recorder at the Old Bailey on the 1st of March, 1866, and, after an abortive attempt by Coleman's counsel to get it adjourned, because Coleman was said to be obtaining important evidence in America, it was tried on Saturday, the 3rd. of March.

Through his counsel, Mr. Montague Chambers, Coleman then pleaded guilty and made a full apology. He said that his letter to *The Times* had not been intended to mean that he could prove the allegation of rape against Sothern, but merely that he was prepared to prove everything connected with Spiritualism. The Deputy Recorder, Thomas Chambers, Common Serjeant and Member of Parliament for Marylebone, then said that Coleman's dispute with Sothern, and his libel against him, "all arose out of a psychological controversy; it gradually grew warmer and warmer; it culminated in a most scandalous libel ... I confess that I am rather disposed to be a believer in Spiritualism, though I never saw anything of it ... This is not a libel prompted by personal and individual malice against Mr. Sothern ... You were gradually provoked into it ... I must mark my sense of the very serious error you committed in overstepping the bounds of philosophical discussion by a personal attack on a private character. You are fined £50."

The same Deputy Recorder had, a month or so earlier, tried a poor woman for a libel against her neighbour, in which she had said the neighbour was "an eternal pest", "an Irish blackguard with a vagabond Scotch husband" and had insinuated that she knew something about some recent robberies. For that libel the defendant had been imprisoned for a month and required to enter into a recognizance for good behaviour.

The press, nationally and provincially, was outraged. Articles appeared in *The Evening Standard, The Morning Herald, The Daily Telegraph, The Morning Star, The Standard, The Liverpool Daily Courier, The Glasgow Daily Herald, The Belfast Northern Whig, The Saturday Review, The Cosmopolitan, The Sunday Times, The Spectator, The Examiner, The Sunday Gazette* and in one or two other magazines, all denouncing the gross disparity between the two sentences and some imputing that the Deputy Recorder had been influenced by his own sympathy with Spiritualism, his concern for his prospects at the next election in Marylebone (where, it was suggested, many Spiritualists lived), and by the social distinction between "a wealthy stockbroker and merchant" and "a poor but foul-mouthed scold". They did not mince their words. One of the shortest articles was in *The Belfast Northern Whig*, but its style and flavour are typical of many of the others –

We have the following from a correspondent:– "The result of 'Lord Dundreary's' case has created very great indignation and dissatisfaction in London. The sentence of the Deputy-Recorder is widely condemned as a scandal on justice. The libel on Mr. Sothern was of the basest and most brutal kind, and the perpetrator of it aggravated his original offence by deliberately sending a letter to the *Times*, in which he said if truth wasn't a libel he would prove that every word of the atrocious charge was true. Having done this, the Spiritualist libeller submits and pleads guilty – that is, pleads guilty to having deliberately circulated as widely as possible a circumstantial charge against Mr. Sothern of having mesmerised a young actress and committed a rape on her, and of having been a notorious and open profligate in other ways. With true wisdom and manliness, Mr. Sothern takes the foul libeller by the throat (metaphorically only, which is possibly to be regretted), and drags him to a court of justice, where the Spiritualist pleads guilty, admits his crime, and declares the falsehood of the charge: and the Deputy-Recorder makes a twaddling and preposterous harangue, in which he more than half admits that he is a Spiritualist himself, and for such an unparalleled outrage inflicts a fine of £50, which is 'immediately paid', the libeller's fellow-spiritualist friends, it is said, contributing the money! Everyone says 'it is monstrous!' and so it really is. Fancy the pain and misery of having to face and repel so infamous an accusation. Fancy the injury done to any man, by being made the object of such a terrible charge, remembering how prone the world is to always take up the evil report against any man, and the awful vitality of a lie!"

The *Morning Star* commented that not only had Coleman "got off very cheaply" but, "so far as can be ascertained, has made a good thing of it" –

There are, it appears, a few members of the Stock Exchange who vary the monotony of watching the market with rapping the tables; and who, after bull-ing and bear-ing time is over, give themselves up to the practices of Spiritualism. Amongst these pillars of commerce a subscription was made for the purpose of defraying the expenses of Coleman's defence, a subscription so good that, if report may be believed, the martyr has a considerable balance in hand. Annoyed at this, and at the fact having gone forth to the world that Mr. Coleman is a stockbroker, certain gentlemen of the Stock Exchange have decided on presenting a testimonial to Mr. Sothern, as a mark of their esteem.

Somebody felt the subject was of sufficient public interest to publish a booklet entitled, *Queen v Coleman. Opinions of the press on the late trial at the Old Bailey before Mr. Thomas Chambers.*